GOLF 1

MEL FLANAGAN GOLF MYSTERIES

THE SECRET OF GOOD GOLF

COUNTRY
HOUSE

Published in 1992 by
Town House and Country House
42 Morehampton Road
Donnybrook
Dublin 4

British Library Cataloguing in Publication Data available from the British Library

ISBN: 0-946172-27-7

Acknowledgements
Photograph on page 24 courtesy of *The Irish Independent*. All the other photographs
were taken by Pat Cashman. The cartoons on pages 39, 64, 76, 90, 106, 120, 124,
127, 129, 144 and 149 are by Clyde Delaney and the remaining illustrations were
drawn by Bill Murphy. The author extends his special thanks to Stephanie Holland
who typed up the original manuscript.

Text editor: Elaine Campion
Design and layout: Bill Murphy
Typeset by Printset & Design Ltd, Dublin
Printed in Ireland by Criterion Press, Dublin

For Imelda, Melvyn, Robbie and Rozanne

'I sometimes wonder whether the likes of me —
I won't say us — can be helped by the likes of
Jack Nicklaus. He cannot have any conception,
fortunately enough for him, of what it feels like
to be me. Tuck a pillow in front of his trousers,
enfeeble his left eye, drain three-quarters of his
strength from his hands and fingers, make him
pant when walking up slopes, and cause the
blood to rush to his head if the ball falls off the
tee and he has to bend down to pick it up
again, and he might begin to get the idea!'

Henry Longhurst
(BBC commentator)

CONTENTS

INTRODUCTORY NOTE

Golf is different from all other sports, indeed it is one of the most testing games you can play. In sports like soccer, rugby, Gaelic football, American football, there is some natural outlet for one's pugnacious instincts, such as strenuous muscular activity, forcing an opponent to the ground, cheering, gesticulating wildly. Not so in golf! It is played in 'cold blood'. David Feherty, Irish Ryder Cup star, once said that the most frustrating thing about golf for him was the fact that the rules of the game did not allow him to crash-tackle his opponent on the golf course.

In golf we are restricted to striking a small stationary ball as hard as we can in the first instance or two, and thereafter playing with a gradually diminishing degree of energy, until such time as almost no effort is required. What is most astonishing is that as the required level of energy decreases, the player's nervous tension increases. Whilst almost no physical effort is required for that three and a half foot side-hill putt, a state of alarming tension permeates the body.

A golfer will always feel bad when he duffs that little chip or misses the tiddler, and he will inevitably carry this depression with him to the next tee. In order to master golf we must 'learn to forget'. We must train ourselves to put our failures behind us and march on afresh to the next challenge. I often call golf the 'one shot in a row game' — once a shot is played, it's over and done with. On to the next...

'Forgetting' between practice sessions is also important. We can all make a fairly decent practice swing — our performance improves dramatically when we are not under pressure,

9

when we are not going for a 'must' shot. We always play our best golf when we allow our 'body' to get on with it, when we do not let negative thoughts and anxieties get in the way. Imagine yourself as two people: one of these people has your present ability in golf, the other is the golfer you would like to become. That is how it is for most of us. Now, try to imagine the two people blending together into one: 'two' no longer exists. This is how it should be. Decide now that you are going to become a good golfer. Adopt a positive, confident approach and ACT AS IF YOU ALREADY ARE A GREAT PLAYER!

You may often have to stand over a shot for quite some time while awaiting your turn. Over-analysis can be detrimental to a player's attempts at improvement. It is a bad idea to study your shots for too long. You should look at the line to the green just *once* before playing your stroke (as you would when putting). Learn to follow your instinct and ignore all the reasons why you feel a particular shot is so important — forget all that rubbish and just play 'instinctive' golf. Trust your first instinct on every shot.

Mel Flanagan
May 1992

GETTING STARTED

THE RIGHT APPROACH

Improving your golf takes time, patience and effort. The fact is, you may initially play a lot worse before you improve! You must be prepared for this.

It is worth remembering the following points:

Adopt a positive attitude

Decide that you are going to become a great player. Act as if you already are a great player. Adopt an 'improving' mentality. Continually imagine yourself striking the ball well. Repeat these words to yourself many times: 'I am a good player', 'I love the game', 'I enjoy practising'.

It is very important that you associate with positive-minded golfers who think like yourself. Avoid negative thinkers. They are everywhere. Do not let the negative attitudes of others destroy your plans for success. Even the way you dress is important. Make no mistake about it, how you look on the outside affects how you feel. If you dress well, you will automatically feel well and play better. Great players all have economy of movement in their swings — they dress neatly, tidily and are very organised. You are what you think you are. Use clothing as a tool to lift your spirits, to build confidence.

Practise to play, don't play to practise

New techniques must be practised. You should not try to digest large amounts of

13

information and then head out onto the golf course with the intention of putting it to the test in your game. This will be disastrous, as on the course you will have only *one* shot with a whole lot depending on it, and probably three impatient golfers waiting for you. So forget it — practise first!

Beat time!

One of the greatest problems in teaching golf is the fact that players never seem to have time to practise between lessons. They are always too busy. You must never allow this to happen to you. Use time in every conceivable way. A simple point — you do not have to be on a practice ground in order to practise. You can practise as you are reading this book! Have a club beside you (preferably an 8 Iron) and work on it as you see the concept that appeals to you. In this way you are schooling yourself to do the basic movement correctly. Your muscles and

Fig 1.1 Practise your swing at home in front of a mirror.

brain will learn together, until the movement becomes 'muscle memory' and your swing instinctive.

Be prepared for setbacks, but wait for the 'magic moments'

A curious fact about the way we progress — when we start to learn anything, especially golf, we never advance steadily. We do not improve gradually. We do it by sudden jerks, by abrupt starts. Then we remain stationary for a time, or we may even slip back and lose some of the ground we had previously gained. These periods of stagnation or retrogression are normal and have been named 'plateaux in the course of learning'. Potentially good golfers will sometimes be stalled for weeks on one of these plateaux. They may be practising hard but cannot get past this brick wall. The weak ones give up in despair. Those with true grit persist, and they find that suddenly, overnight, without their knowing how or why, it has happened, they have made great progress. They have lifted from the plateau like an aeroplane. Abruptly they have found the knack. Have the patience to wait for these magic moments!

Good things do not happen by accident! I have for many years observed golfers practising — those who have succeeded are not as a general rule players of extraordinary ability. Rather, they have been endowed with persistence and dogged determination. They kept on. They arrived.

Go 'first class' on your equipment

Pay twice as much — buy half as many. Buy clubs that complement your game. Remember, the Driver is a very important club. I see so many people with totally unsuitable Drivers, so rigid, heavy and straight-faced that even tournament players would have trouble breaking 80 with them.

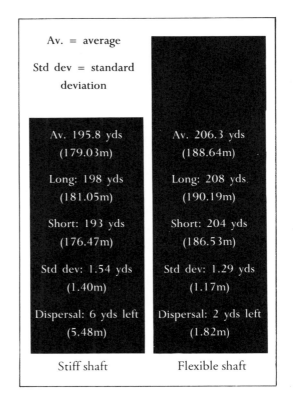

Fig 1.2 When buying your Driver, bear in mind that you can gain extra distance if the shaft is flexible.

Av. = average

Std dev = standard deviation

Stiff shaft	Flexible shaft
Av. 195.8 yds (179.03m)	Av. 206.3 yds (188.64m)
Long: 198 yds (181.05m)	Long: 208 yds (190.19m)
Short: 193 yds (176.47m)	Short: 204 yds (186.53m)
Std dev: 1.54 yds (1.40m)	Std dev: 1.29 yds (1.17m)
Dispersal: 6 yds left (5.48m)	Dispersal: 2 yds left (1.82m)

An easy-to-use Driver is what you should be looking for — one that is lofted, light, and not too stiff in the shaft. The lightness will make it easy to swing, the whippier shaft will add extra distance, and the loft will keep the ball on line by creating back-spin rather than side-spin.

Do not fall into the trap of doing your final exam first

I always remember a player who came to me in the driving range and said: 'I want to learn the game of golf.' I noticed he had only one club with him — a Driver. I enquired if he had any other clubs. He said no. His theory was simply this: the Driver is the most difficult club, so if he mastered that one, the rest would come easy. I explained to him the perils of 'trying to do the final exam first', that he wasn't in the range for exercise, rather to learn a basic technique.

EQUIPMENT

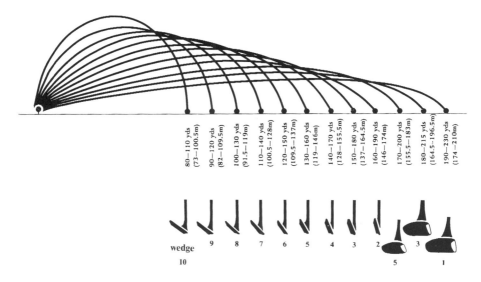

| 80—110 yds (73—100.5m) | 90—120 yds (82—109.5m) | 100—130 yds (91.5—119m) | 110—140 yds (100.5—128m) | 120—150 yds (109.5—137m) | 130—160 yds (119—146m) | 140—170 yds (128—155.5m) | 150—180 yds (137—164.5m) | 160—190 yds (146—174m) | 170—200 yds (155.5—183m) | 180—215 yds (164.5—196.5m) | 190—230 yds (174—210m) |

wedge   9   8   7   6   5   4   3   2   3

10   5   1

Fig 1.3 This diagram shows the distances that both professional and handicap golfers can expect to achieve with individual clubs.

Clubs

You are allowed only fourteen clubs. The choice of clubs is entirely up to yourself.

The Woods generally run from No. 1 to No. 5, the Irons from No. 2 to Sand-wedge (No. 11).

The Woods from No. 1 to 5, and the Irons from No. 2 to 6 are the really difficult clubs to use. A Driver or No. 1, unless made to order, has an 11 degree loft; the face is very flat.

You should look at the markings on the sole plate of the Woods and by the lines you will know if you are an 'out to in' or an 'in to out' swinger. You could double check this by looking at the Irons, and from the markings on the face you will see what part of the club 'meets' the ball. You should also look at

18

the Woods and check the paint to see if you are using a steep swing and chipping the paint on the top of the head. Pupils never believe me when I tell them that they are hitting the ball near the shank of the Iron. I mark the back of the ball with chalk, and this chalk mark is transferred onto the clubface at impact. Immediately they can see if it's too near the shank of the clubhead. You should try this experiment for yourself.

The golf-ball

In my opinion, despite the advertising claims, there is not much difference in the distance you will get from balls of comparable quality. Tests conducted by the US Golf Association showed that no brand is appreciably superior to its several nearest competitors.

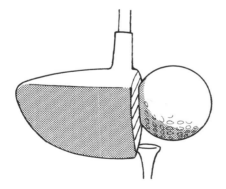

Fig 1.4 The distance a ball will travel is determined by the strength of impact between clubhead and ball.

The distance a ball will carry is governed by how much it is compressed and its ability to snap back when struck. This will depend on how hard the ball is and how hard it is struck. To increase your driving distance, think of compressing the ball a little bit more than you normally do at impact.

Modern balls range from 100 compression to 60. 100 is suitable for hard hitters, while average players should use 80 to 90. Compression increases in cold conditions and decreases in heat. This is why you should play with a softer ball in the winter.

A golf-ball may not weigh more than 1.62 ounces (45.92g) or be less than 1.68 inches (4.26cm) in diameter.

The earliest golf-balls were made of hardwood or ivory. These were followed by balls stuffed with feathers, and later by the gutta percha ball, filled with a rubber-like substance. Later balls had rubber liquid or steel centres wound up with stretched rubber bands and balata (a type of gum). Today golf-balls are solid and cut-proof. Aerodynamics of 336 dimples and back-spin of from 2000 to 8000 r.p.m. (revolutions per minute) keep the ball airborne for twice as long as a ball with a smooth surface.

The speed with which the ball leaves the face of the Driver when struck by a good golfer is about 170 m.p.h (273.5 km.p.h). The high-compression ball is in contact with the clubface for 4/10,000 of a second. The softer ball stays on the clubface longer and, therefore, it can be controlled better.

UNDERSTAND THE BASICS

Grip 'softly' and swing 'easy'

Look at the grip on the shaft of the clubs. The markings on the grip will reveal if the club is moving too much in your swing. If you are wearing your grips a lot, you are gripping the club too tightly, swinging too much with your hands and too fast. Your game will improve a lot if you respect your grips. It is important not to 'strangle' the club with your hands. No matter how lightly you hold the club it will always 'firm' up when the ball goes down and you make a swing at it. On the other hand, if you grip very tightly at address, it will ease on the take-away. It will always be a fast right side take-away which immediately loosens at the top, and you will lose control through the hitting area.

The cure is to grip very loosely as if the club was going to 'fly' out of your hands, and practise hitting half the distance with a full swing. Feel your arms are swinging, not just your hands and wrists. In other words, move your whole left side back while you keep your strong right side quiet on the backswing.

Fig 1.5 Tightening your grip will <u>not</u> result in greater distance.

Avoid the 'V' swing

To solve the mystery of golf, you must understand the geometry involved. What is the first aim of the swing? What are you trying to do? The first aim of your golf swing is to move the ball forwards — down the fairway.

The force or power of your swing with the club must be applied from 'behind', towards the back of the ball. This seems easy, but it is actually very difficult to do. Why?

Fig 1.6 Avoid the 'V' swing. This illustration demonstrates the effect of the 'V' swing, and the more acceptable wide sweeping swing. The wide swing doubles your distance.

1. We have to stand on one side of the ball (over it) as we prepare to move it forwards. We are in a very steep position over the ball at address. We would much prefer if we were allowed to stand behind it.

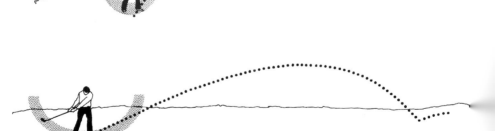

2. Unfortunately we make the ball the 'focal' point of the swing. As we swing the club farther back, we inevitably swing it higher and higher, so as we change direction and swing forwards, a major thought in our mind is to strike a good shot. What we are concentrating on is the ball on the

ground. The actual clubhead has reached a height of six feet (almost 2m) at the top of the backswing. Many golfers take the direct route down, straight down — the 'V' swing. This is much easier to do. What we *should* do is 'bottom' the clubhead first, then swing it forwards. Swing wide and easy into the back of the ball. Do not swing directly to the ball from the top. Do not swing 'at', swing 'through' the ball.

3. The right-hand side of your upper body is more developed, which lends itself to a stronger right-hand grip and a lifting action — steep backswing.

4. We associate a long drive with power. We grip tighter and snatch the club with hands and wrists only — a 'lottery' swipe at the ball.

In the driving range, many golfers practise mistakes — usually one or other variety of the 'V' swing.

The 'correct' golf swing

Let us look at what happens in other sports in a dead-ball situation, for example, converting a try in rugby or taking a corner kick in soccer. Let us study the action, the angles that are used.

The player, once he has placed the ball on the ground, goes back at an 'inside angle' and runs in from this 'inside angle'; he swings his foot from an inside-out angle as he strikes the ball. He does not run straight back and would never consider an outside run.

Fig 1.7 In trying to achieve the 'inside out' angle in the downswing, you are looking for the same angle as that which good rugby players use.

A good golf swing uses similar angles. I call it the 'L' turn. A backward and forward movement. A bald factual statement. At

address you stand ABOVE a golf-ball. You must school yourself to swing BEHIND the ball, at a slight angle — like the rugby or soccer player — and on swinging forwards, always swing the clubhead in shallow from behind and extend your arms on the follow-through. Wide, Wide, Wide!

The difference between the good and the bad swing is simply that in the bad swing the clubhead is descending sharply on the ball, while in the good swing the clubhead is sweeping in along to the ground.

Turn the 'L' and break out of the 'V' forever. Look after the 'middle' of your swing.

On the practice ground:
Have a short-range attainable goal, for example, a 100-yard (90m) accurate shot.

Use an 8 Iron, tee the ball up, use a very short swing. Above all, grip lightly and hit the ball softly. 'Caress' the little ball down the fairway.

GOOD SWING THOUGHTS — repeat to yourself:

'No wrists. Dead hands.'

'I know I am standing *above* the ball.'

'I am going to turn *behind* the ball.'

'I am going to strike the *back* of the ball.'

'I am going to move *through* the impact area.'

I am going to extend my arms out after impact, ensuring a *wide* follow-through.'
25

Reading ball flight

The height of your shots is dictated by your plane of swing.

If your shots are too high, your swing plane is steep. You are contacting the ball much too low, coming down on it. This steepness creates excess back-spin, causing the ball to rise up very high and drop down a short

Fig 1.8 A steep swing causes low contact, and this creates excessive back-spin and a high shot.

distance away. So the height is due to the angle of your attack or the actual part of the ball you strike — top, middle, bottom.

If your swing-plane is too flat (rounded), your shots will fly much too low, as this plane contacts the ball much higher up. The part of the ball — top, middle, bottom — is very important. If you wish to strike a low ball, aim for the top half of the ball. I call it a top-the-egg shot. If you want more height, aim lower down on the ball.

Shot elevation required	The ball
High	Low contact (back-spin/steep swing)
Low	High contact (flat swing)

Fig 1.9 If the clubhead contacts the top of the ball, it will have a very low flight.

In the sand

You should use your feet as 'educators' when you have to play a shot from the sand. By 'shuffling' your feet you will be able to gauge for yourself the density of the sand. (See Chapter 6, Fig 6.10.) Remember, the ball will come out much faster from hard sand than from soft sand. If you feel that the sand is soft, you must play a much firmer shot, aiming to send the ball past the pin. If the sand is hard, play an easier shot.

27

Fig 1.10

① Eyes focusing behind ball: *This focus will help direct the swing towards the back of the ball. Also helps shoulder turn.*

② Arms hanging freely: *If you were asked to lift an object off the ground, you would move in nearly on top of it and 'lever' it up with your arms. You would never attempt to lift at full stretch.*

③ Left arm extended: *Creates wide arc to swing. Consistency comes when your left arm becomes an 'extension of the shaft'.*

④ Left shoulder tilted up: *Helps create a similar position at impact — right moves down as left moves up (an upswing hit).*

⑤ Right elbow tucked in: *Helps flat shoulder turn. Weakens the 'bully' strong right arm. Helps player get inside the ball early in the backswing.*

⑥ Weight back on right foot: *Much easier to get behind the ball.*

Closed stance: *Encourages 'in to out' swing. Swing along feet line.*

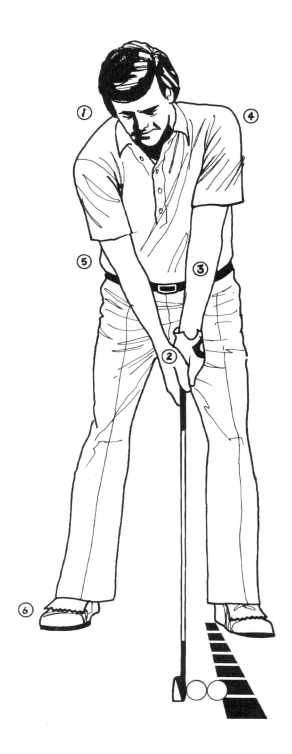

28

Address and impact

When you address the ball, you are making
a statement. You are saying: 'This is the
position I would like to be in when I strike
the ball.' It is the same in every swing, good
or bad. You will always tend to return to
your address position at impact.

When the great players wish to alter the
flight of their shots they do so by changing
their address position, that is, by standing
more open or more closed or.....

The point is, you may feel a fault in the
hitting area which is caused by your swing,
but it originated way back in your set-up.
The correction is also to be found there.
From setting up to impact takes
approximately 1.5 seconds. If you are able to
position yourself like a top-class player, you
have a very good chance of returning to this
position at impact.

What you do in the set-up will determine
how you will be at impact, and if you wish
to improve impact, you must first of all
improve your position at address. As sure as
night follows day, a sound set-up is followed
by a good swing.

Here is a routine you can practise at home:

Stand erect, place club in fingers of your left hand and close so that the 'V' formed by thumb and base of index finger points to right shoulder. (See Figs 1.11 and 1.12.) Extend your left arm fully. Widen stance to shoulder width. Hold your back straight up, stick your rear end out and move your weight back onto your heels. Flex your knees and hips in order to get down to the ball. Lift up your chin and turn your head to the right.

Fig 1.11 The correct way to place your left hand on the grip.

Place your right arm behind your back. Drop your right shoulder down and, using an underarm movement, place your right hand on the club so that the 'V' formed by your thumb and index finger points in the same direction as the 'V' on the left hand (towards right shoulder). Flex your right elbow inwards. This movement ensures that your stronger right arm is placed in a totally submissive position. Even though right now you may feel like an octopus, you should begin to look like the set-up shown in Fig 1.16.

Fig 1.12 Place the left hand on the grip so that the 'V' formed by the base of your index finger and thumb points in the direction of your right shoulder.

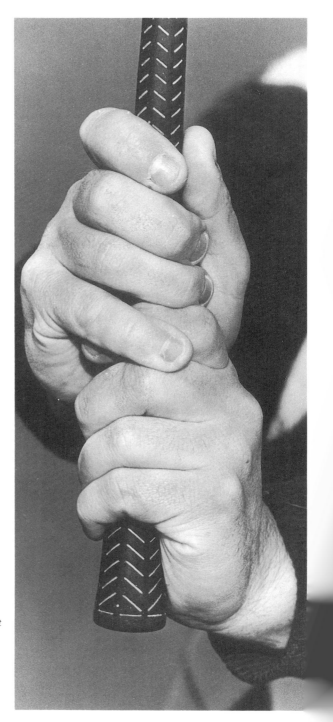

Fig 1.13 Ninety-two per cent
of all professionals use this
grip. It is known as the
'Vardon overlap'. Give it a
try.

1.14

TUCK IN
RIGHT
ELBOW

Practise your set-up at
home
*Fig 1.14 Tuck in right
elbow*
Fig 1.15 Right arm relaxed
Fig 1.16 Strengthen left arm

1.16

STRENGTHEN
LEFT ARM.

1.15

RIGHT ARM RELAXED

Set-up

People often ask me how I manage to change a golfer's swing, especially if his next game is at the weekend and the new swing has to work immediately! The truth is, I rarely ever have to change any player's swing. Rather, I change the set-up. I set up a whole series of different angles, angles that will guarantee a different result. In a matter of minutes I could 'set the player up' to slice, hook, sky, etc.

Any golfer who habitually slices the ball right (see Fig 1.17) will naturally fear the right-hand side and therefore aim 'away off' to the left (see Fig 1.18). This is a very human reaction. Usually when we want something to go left, for example our car, we aim to the left. The difference between the car and the golf-ball is that the car is not 'spinning' as well as moving. A golf-ball on the other hand, if it is struck left with an open clubface (pointing right), will eventually succeed in 'worming' its way to the right — every time. My advice to someone who slices the ball is this: you must attack the right-hand side of the fairway. You must change your attitude and no longer 'fear' the right — instead you must attack it. This works because golf is a game of opposites.

The golfer who hooks the ball (see Fig 1.19) will always aim away from the trouble (see Fig 1.20). I change this golfer's grip to the angle shown in Fig 1.21 and his stance to an open one (see Fig 1.18). The result: the shots begin to move in the desired direction (correcting the out-of-control hook) (see Fig 1.17).

1.17

Your set-up will affect your swing

Fig 1.17 This shows the slice off to the right of the green.

Fig 1.18 If you slice to the right you will automatically aim to the left in an effort to save the shot.

Fig 1.19 This shows the hook off to the left of the green.

Fig. 1.20 The golfer who hooks to the left will inevitably aim to the right.

Fig 1.21 To correct the hook, change the grip angle so that the 'V' between the base of your index finger and thumb points towards your chin, and aim to the left. This is called the 'weak grip'.

1.18

1.19

1.20

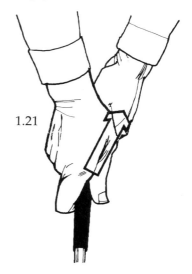

1.21

These changes are all made at set-up, as your grip angle controls your clubface angle at impact and your feet alignment controls your swing-line. This is why this early and rather tedious lesson is so important.

Some good advice

Set up sequential short-range goals
The secret for you now is to set up small, sequential short-range goals that are attainable, for example, instead of starting at the beginning, why not start at the end? Think of this: 65 per cent of golf is played within thirty yards (27m) of the green! We all feel (even on our worst day!) that we have the ability to strike the ball thirty yards. If we develop the technique to strike the ball accurately to the flag from thirty yards in, we will have only 35 per cent of the game left to conquer. To explain further, 43 per cent (of the 65 per cent) of the total shots you take are not on the course but on the green. In this part of the game, the ball does not actually leave the ground at all!

Count your putts
Have you ever counted your putts? If your average is three and a half putts per hole as a beginner, your total putts would amount to sixty-three. I know you can become a damn good putter — why not set yourself a simple goal? It demands absolutely no physical effort. Bring your average down to two putts per hole or thirty-six per round. If you succeed you have, in one simple move, knocked twenty-seven shots off what is considered the average score for a beginner.

Plus, think of the overall confidence it will bring to your game, and of the fear that this talent will strike into the hearts of your opponents! The great players spend 60 per cent of their practice time on their short game, the novice an average of 15 per cent! The legendary Scottish golfer Willie Park once said: 'A golfer who can putt is a match for anyone. A golfer who can't is a match for nobody!'

Observe your divots
The divot shown in Fig 1.22 indicates a swing path that is towards the left or 'out to in'. This shows that the ball is going to at least start left and will stay left or veer to the right, depending on the club you are using and the direction in which the clubface is pointing at impact.

To correct this, simply align the clubhead more to the right. Ensure that your left-hand grip is turned to the right (stronger grip). Align your feet, hips and shoulders to right. Swing along to the line of the body and make sure that you release the clubhead — do not let the body go with it.

If the divot is 'going the other way' or is straight towards the target, you are in much better shape. If the ball is still not hitting the target it is because your clubface is not pointing at the target at impact — even though you are swinging in the direction of the target. It is 'open' or 'closed'. You have to check that the face is square to where you want the ball to go.

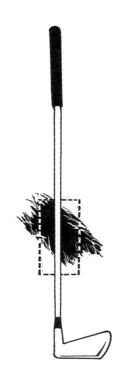

Fig 1.22 You will inevitably play bad golf if your divots look like this. The dotted line shows the correct divot line, going in the direction of the target.

Etiquette

Respect your club's rules and the earth.

Fig 1.23 Replace divots

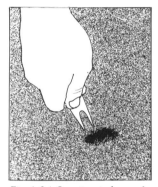

Fig 1.24 Repair pitch marks

Fig 1.25 Repair footprints in a bunker

'YOU DON'T MEAN...'
A friend of mine, Jack, told me an amazing story of something that happened to him. He is quite religious. He went to confession and the priest started off by saying, 'Well son, tell me your sins.'

'Bless me Father for I have sinned,' Jack confessed. 'I have used terrible language. I have taken the Lord's name in vain.' The priest said, 'Son, tell me when did this happen.' Jack replied, 'On the golf course, Father.' 'Oh, I see. I'm a keen golfer myself — maybe you would like to explain how it happened.' Jack continued, 'You see Father, I was playing in the Captain's Prize. I had a wonderful round of golf going after seventeen holes. Some of my friends came out from the clubhouse and told me that all I needed was a par to win it.'

The priest brought his head forward. He was now listening intently. 'Okay, so you knocked the ball out of bounds off the tee?' 'No, Father, that's the infuriating part,' said Jack, getting slightly irritated. 'I struck the most perfect drive, right down the middle, almost 290 yards (265m), but when I arrived, if I didn't find the ball lying over a heel mark!' 'Okay,' said Father, 'you

opening the face even more, and chopped down with the open face from the outside. The ball rose almost vertically and it dropped like a butterfly with a sore foot, fifteen inches from the hole.'

'You don't mean,' Father said heatedly, 'that you missed the ★★★★ putt!'

swore violently.' 'No, no Father! I held my composure.' (Father's head was now leaning onto the mesh separating the two of them.)

Jack went on. 'I have a beautiful 5 Wood — metal head — with a gold shaft. I visualised the ball flying like a rocket towards the green, out of the heel mark....' 'Go on.' 'Well, Father, I played the ball slightly back in my stance, took a steeper back-swing, stayed down in on the shot and played the most wonderful 5 Wood I think I ever played.'

Father was looking at him weirdly now. 'But you won't believe what happened,' said Jack. (Father was almost relieved.) 'When the ball landed, it must have struck something. If it didn't ricochet off at a terrible angle into that bunker in front of the green — you know the one I mean — the ball finished right up under the lip, an unplayable ball, Father!' 'So that's where you used the foul, abusive language,' said Father, moving back from the mesh.

'No, no, no, Father!' (Father's head lurched back again.) 'I have a sand wedge for seventeen years, a favourite old club of mine. I held my composure — visualised the perfect explosion shot. I flattened out the face of the sand wedge. I dug my feet really well into the sand. I took the club up most steeply, 39

CONSISTENCY IN PLAY

Golfers who decide they want to improve through tuition usually give similar answers to these questions:

Why have you come for a lesson?
What's your problem?
What would you like to work on during this half hour?

Their answers are usually some variation of: 'Well, the situation is that I can hit a great shot, even a corker, but I can never manage to repeat it consistently. I would love to be consistent.'

Do you want to know the secret of consistency?

Let's start by answering these questions:

1. *Are your shots generally too high and lack distance? Are you a short hitter?*

2. *Do you occasionally slice, pull, top, sky, shank shots?*

3. *Are you afraid to tee the ball high? Do you use a very low tee? (If so, you are protecting a bad swing.)*

4. *Are your divots going leftwards?*

5. *Are you unable to hit a 3 Iron to its full, or have you a suspect long game but an adequate short game?*

6. *Do you strike the 6 Iron and 3 Iron the same distance?*

If you answer 'Yes' to any or all of these questions, then your swing is off-plane and out of tempo (much too fast).

Consistency has to do with a slow, even tempo and a flat, wide swing-plane.

▶ TEMPO AND SWING-PLANE

Tempo and swing-plane are closely related to one another and, more importantly, to consistent shots. Think of tempo for a moment. If you drive your car slowly you may not arrive as fast as you would wish, but it is unlikely that you will have an accident on the way. In fact, if you do anything slowly you are less likely to make mistakes. The same principle applies to golf — a hurried swing will be an inconsistent one, and will give you a variety of results. A hurried swing is certain to be off-plane and much too steep — the dreaded 'V' type.

Golfers do not swing off-plane and out of tempo deliberately. They do so because of a) the mistaken idea that speed equals distance — the faster I swing, the further the ball will go (it's very hard to swing easy!), and b) the fact that our bodies contain big and small muscles. Our legs, arms and shoulders are the bigger ones, our hands and wrists the smaller ones. When we look for distance, especially with the Driver, our hands and wrists take over. High handicap golfers grip the club much too tightly — they strangle the club. You must always remember that your hands are transmitters of power — you create power in your body and transmit this power through your hands down to the clubhead at impact. A tight grip blocks this transfer.

The smaller muscles have the ability to move much faster than the arms and the shoulders — they tend to race away in the backswing. You must realise that your hands and wrists are very flexible, and capable of sudden movement. Quick sudden movements are very hard to control. Have you ever watched a great player strike the ball? Were you amazed by his/her easy tempo? The great players, from many years' experience, have learned to control their swings with the bigger muscles — the arms and shoulders. Because these muscles move much slower than the hands and wrists, they are much easier to control. These players are therefore able to consistently repeat the same swing time and again.

Quick, small muscle movements also lead to a steep, chopping swing. The simple reason why a golfer mistakenly swings too fast is because he/she is allowing the smaller muscles to take over the swing — a snatch with the hands, a quick break with the wrists. This smaller muscle movement is of course much easier to do. We prefer it. This incorrect small muscle movement will always resemble the 'V' shape, and of course be out of plane, as the quick snatch with the wrists will always prevent the 'body turn' from taking place. There is simply no time for the body to actually turn away.

Fig 2.1 Many golfers lift the
club up steeply in the
backswing, making a 'V'
swing. This is incorrect. In
order to drive the ball
forwards you must learn to
turn your back to the target
before you lift your arms.

PLAY WITH 'DEAD HANDS'

To become consistent you must school yourself into deadening your smaller muscles — your hands and wrists — and developing a relaxed tempo by rotating the 'L' back as a unit. Turn your back on the target (see the drills at the end of this chapter). I call this the 'package deal', whereby everything turns together, with the knees resisting. This way you are on-plane with a nice easy tempo. You must learn to turn 'behind' the ball.

This 'package deal' is sometimes referred to as the 'connection theory' because the clubhead is connected to your left arm and shoulder — you should always move the shoulder, arm and clubhead as one unit.

2.2 The flatter swing is best.
The golfer must swing
'inside' the pane of glass.

a)

A special relationship should exist between your belly button and the top of the shaft throughout the swing. The club must never escape from the body (belly button) in the good swing. It should always be in sync with the body.

I have a saying I use during lessons: 'If you develop a flat swing, you will end up with a fat wallet. If you have a steep swing, you will always have a thin wallet!' In other words, you are on to a winner with the flat swing — the steep swing is for losers. (See Fig 2.2.)

Avoid a 'tilty' shoulder turn. School yourself into turning your shoulders at the same level. Turn your back on the target. Move your left shoulder out and right shoulder back behind you as your start your backswing. Concentrate on the shoulder plane. Your shoulders turn while your knees

2.3 This rotary drill shows the correct positions for:
a) ADDRESS — facing the ball
b) BACKSWING — turn your back to the target
c) FINISHING SWING — face to target

c)

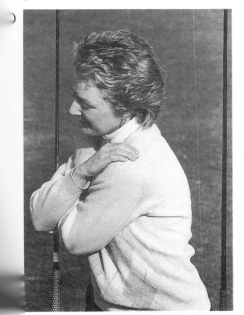

resist. The reasons why you must turn are a) to set up a shallow angle whereupon you can attack the back of the ball and drive it forwards, and b) to create power. You must learn to turn your left side into your right side.

THE ROTARY SWING

Body pivot is essential for consistency. This is achieved through the rotary swing (see Fig 2.3). This works because:

1. The ball is static.
2. Your body is static.

Hammer throwers, for example, use this rotation theory whereby their shoulders rotate at right angles to their spines. Similarly, the 'body turn' plays a most important part in the golf swing. You must learn to hit the ball with your complete body, and avoid a quick swipe with your hands and wrists whilst your body remains rigid.

THE FORWARD SWING

If you thought it was difficult to sort out your backswing plane, allow me to let you in on another little secret — it is much more difficult to swing on-plane on your downswing. You must school yourself into swinging wider on your downswing than you do on your backswing. Unfortunately, most golfers swing very steep on their downswing. This is because when you swing the clubhead back it reaches a height of six feet (almost 2m) off the ground and the ball is two inches (5cm) off the ground. It has been calculated that it takes a fifth of a second for the clubhead to come from the height of six feet down to two inches, that is, from the top of the backswing to impact. When you are up in the top of your backswing, what you see (unfortunately) is the ball. For the downswing you must learn not to swing directly to the ball, rather to swing your clubhead on a shallower plane than you would on your backswing. Score a goal rather than a point (see Fig 2.4).

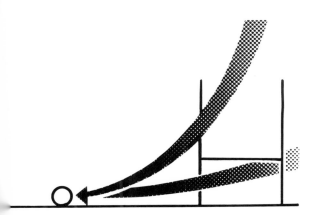

Fig 2.4 Score a goal rather than a point.

47

The better players give themselves enough time to strike the back of the ball. Good golfers 'detour' their downswings, that is, they swing the clubhead down into a shallower position first, *then* they swing it forwards. If you swing into a shallower position, the first advantage is that when the clubhead is coming in towards the back of the ball it will be travelling more or less parallel to the ground. But if you don't 'bottom out' your club, the clubhead will travel very steeply downwards at impact. The power of the swing will then go into the ground.

▶ RESIST THE POWER SYNDROME

Just before impact a thought usually comes into our minds — to give the ball a little bit more power so as to increase the pace and gain a bit extra on distance. Oscar Wilde once remarked: 'I can resist anything but temptation.' Avoid the power syndrome, no matter how tempted you may be.

If you swing wide going back, you have secured a good angle to attack the back of the ball — you must therefore take advantage of the situation you have created. If you succeed in going back low (wide), swing in on the same plane and extend your arms out after impact — in other words, repeat backswing and forward-swing planes. My message is: something good must happen on either side of the ball! Think 'wide, wide, wide

Force is simply a killer in the downswing. Stay 'behind' the ball. Slow down your swing effort before impact. From the top of your backswing your hands have to travel

Fig 2.5 Aggressive swings, aimed at achieving distance, are counter-productive. Here the player is hitting with the handle, resulting in an impact position in which the handle is pointing forwards and the clubhead is lagging behind — an inevitable slice.

approximately three feet (1m) in order for them to reach level with the ball, while the clubhead has to travel approximately nine feet (3m). Therefore your hands have to travel one third of the distance of the clubhead. The clubhead is on the outer extremity and the hands are on the inner extremity. If you decide to apply a little

49

Fig 2.6 Wait for the clubhead to catch up with your hands. Diagram shows the short distance the hands have to travel compared to the clubhead.

more force and move your body forward, your hands will automatically move faster through the impact area, so the clubhead will lag even further behind. The clubhead will also come down very steeply on the ball.

You must activate the clubhead. It is very important to keep on your own side of the 'road' — not to swing down and across, rather to swing down on the inside and thereafter out through the ball — from inside out. Get the feeling of swinging the club on-plane from the top of the backswing in towards the back of the ball. If you want to be a good golfer, you must allow your club to go down and out. Stay 'inside' before
50 impact.

AVOID THE 'BAD' SHOTS

There are only nine possible bad shots in golf. If you swing from outside, you will make an 'out to in' swing, and this may result in any or all of the following six bad shots.

If you swing off-plane on your downswing (that is, steep), you will be swinging at the ball from outside and across the swing-line. The most likely result of this is the *slice shot* — the clubhead will be coming from out to in and will be slightly open to the swing-line. This is a problem for 75 per cent of golfers.

Then there is the *pull shot* where the clubface is square to the swing-line and the ball goes straight to the left.

As the clubhead is descending very sharply it is possible that you may actually come down on 'top' of the ball — this is called a *top shot*.

As the clubhead is coming off-plane, down towards the ball, it is also possible that you may hit the bottom of the ball and 'sky' it into the air — a *sky shot*.

Because the clubhead is coming down very steeply, it may 'fluff' into the ground — this is referred to as a *fluff shot*.

With the Iron shot, especially up around the green, if you swing outside on the downswing, the clubhead may not make contact with the ball at all. It will be the 'shank' of the club that will hit the ball — a so-called *shank shot*.

Some people like to swing a little bit off-plane on their backswings, but you must learn to swing on-plane as you come into the ball. The common denominator of every great player is that they are right at impact, irrespective of how they get there, and every

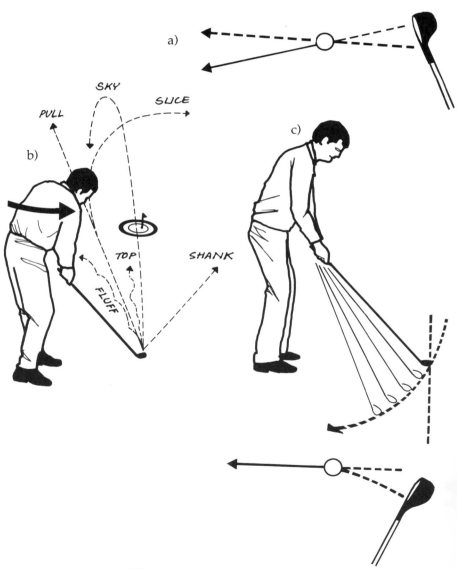

one of them hits the ball from the *inside*.
They arrive into a position where the
clubhead is coming in on a shallow plane,
where the right elbow is brushing off their
side (right hip). If you can learn to get into
this area on your downswing, you will have
eliminated 75 per cent of the bad shots.

Let me tell you a secret of golf, a way in
which it is nearly impossible to hit a bad
shot: you must start by deadening the
muscles in your hands and wrists and
schooling yourself to swing on-plane, turning
the 'L', starting your forward swing by
rotating your left hip out of the way, thus

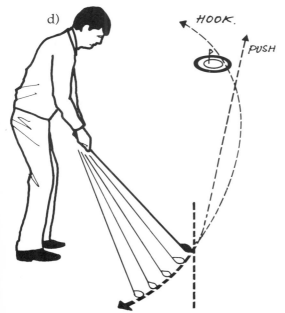

reating clubhead speed, and then
pproaching from the inside towards the
ack of the ball, extending your arms out
ter impact. In other words, you have to
ork your bigger muscles to swing them on-
ane and try to swing on a shallower plane
the downswing than on the backswing.

► SWING TIPS

Turn flat on your backswing but don't swing flat as you follow through. From my experience, the most common mistakes that practising golfers make are: a) failure to turn their shoulders in the backswing (to get 'inside', to get an angle on the ball), b) swinging down and across the line through impact.

Fig 2.8 Right elbow to right hip is the first move on the downswing. This results in the correct 'inside' position.

Let there be absolutely no doubt about it — swinging across the line is the biggest fault in the game. You must remember the following (an amazing piece of information you might say!): your arms are attached to your shoulders! So much so that they do not like going away from them. I cringe when I see the swings of so many potentially good players collapsing leftwards at impact. When I say 'turn flat — don't swing flat', what I

mean is that the most important part of the swing happens AFTER you strike the golf-ball. You must school yourself into swinging wide on your follow-through. Force your arms out after impact, extend the triangle down the line and stop halfway into your follow-through. Check your left arm — has it collapsed too early? I am not suggesting you finish your full swing with your two arms in a fully extended position. I am saying, widen your follow-through before you relax your arms at the end. Lock it to the target.

Another tip — once you have pin-pointed your target, forget about where it actually is. While in the practice area look at another (imaginary) target — well right of the real one. Lock your follow-through 'out' to this one. It's an 'optical illusion' you must perform. Swing right of where you want the ball to go. Because your arms are attached to your shoulders, if you don't do this 'imaginary' right swing, you will find yourself swinging left of the target.

Fig 2.9 To achieve consistency you must learn to extend your arms outwards after impact. Swing to the right, to an imaginary target. This will result in a wide follow-through.

SWING ARMS TO RIGHT OF TARGET

I often think that hitting a drive off a tee is like taking the ball on the fly! Imagine that the ball has been tossed to you and you must take it on the fly before it hits the ground. Think of the sweeping swing you would use. In the same way, you must learn to sweep the ball away off the tee.

▶ THE IMPORTANCE OF T-E-M-P-O

Rotate in tempo: It is very hard to swing 'easy'!

I remember giving a lesson to a player who had a steep swing that was also quick and jerky. He was demanding distance as a right and was very inconsistent. I jokingly said to him: 'Do you know you are supposed to smile as you strike, not grimace.' I also said: 'Imagine your nick-name is S-M-O-O-T-H-I-E, that you have a smooth swing, and just think of driving the ball a short distance.' His tempo and plane improved dramatically, as did his consistency. Have the confidence to hit the ball softly.

Learn to use an 8 Iron tempo with your Driver. Don't look for distance. Let it come to you. As the saying goes, 'Don't force the feel', rather 'feel the force'. Allow your tempo and an accurate strike to do the job. I often compare a golf swing with driving a pin into wood with a hammer. The pin is so delicate — if you strike it too hard, you will bend it. You must give it just the right amount — an accurate strike with an even tempo.

Remember, the golf swing is one continuous motion, a repeating rotating swing, respecting angles and pace.

Fig 2.10 Don't force the feel, feel the force.

56

Fig 2.11 In order to achieve maximum distance with minimum effort you must learn to hit the ball with your Driver only on the upswing.

▶ DRILLS

Practice routine 1
Power posture
1. Squat
2. Stick out your rear end

Practise hitting 'soft' shots with a half-swing. Widen the middle of your swing. Get rid of the 'V' swing forever.

Power creation
3. Transfer and turn your upper body against the resistance of your knees — the foundation of the swing. (See Fig 2.12(b).)

Power release on shallow plane
4. Rotate the left hip. (See Fig 2.12(c).)
5. Finish with the middle of your belt facing the target.
6. Extend your two arms out after impact ('Package deal').

Use rotation to help create clubhead speed. Use an 8 Iron and tee a dozen balls in a row. Practise 'pushing' the ball forwards eighty yards (75m) using the half-swing, finishing with arms fully extended in the triangle position.

Practise the above drills as often as you can, with or without a club. The famous American instructor Gene O'Brien once said: 'I shall always stress that it is quite easy to hit a golf-ball consistently after you have taught yourself how to swing a golf club away from the ball.'

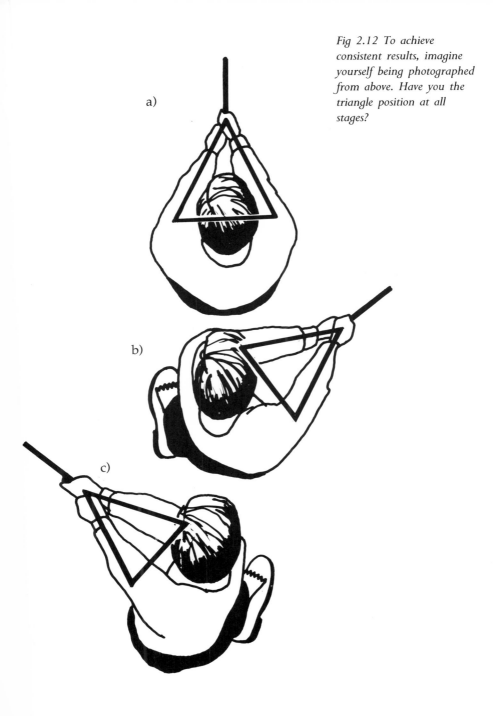

a)

b)

c)

Fig 2.12 To achieve consistent results, imagine yourself being photographed from above. Have you the triangle position at all stages?

59

Keep saying the following to yourself as you practise your swing:

'I am standing above.'
'I must turn behind (back to target).'
'Hit the back of the ball.'
'Move through (clear left side).'
'Finish with my arms in the triangle position.'

Fig 2.13 If you hit the ball on the upswing, you will get a clean hit and maximum distance.

Practice routine 2

Do the following drill:

- Develop a swing with a forward momentum.
- Flatten the middle of your swing. (See Fig 1.6.)
- Place one golf-ball on the ground, another ball on the tee. (See Fig 2.13.)
- Sweep clubhead over the ball on the tee at full speed.
- Memorise that 'feel' and use it while striking.
- Learn to sweep the clubhead up as you strike.

60

I call this the 'Hit it up to heaven' drill. The secret of drive is to 'nearly' top the ball. Remember, there is no bottom to the good swing. You are at an unfortunate angle at address. You are standing above the ball. Normally when you wish to move anything forwards, you place your body behind that object.

Fig 2.14 Don't make the ball the focal point of your swing. It must be incidental to your swing.

SUMMARY

The big thing in golf is to move behind the ball on the backswing and hold the shallow angle through the swing — don't give it away. The secret is to recognise a bad angle at address and to do something about it. Create an angle of attack where you can strike the back of the ball.

I often feel that the ball occupies a huge place in the beginner's mind. The whole swing, every sinew, all thoughts, are centred around getting that ball away. Doubts exist as to whether the club will contact it, hit it a distance, slice it or not. It is as if there is a brick wall just behind the ball and a great effort is made right up to impact, but the swing suddenly collides with the wall and stops right there. No follow-through.

In the better players' swing, the body tension and anxiety is not as dominant. The distance hit is not as crucial. Good players swing 'past' the ball, as if it was not there — sweep through it smoothly. They avoid hitting at the ball — they move through it. I remember watching Ian Woosnam hit shots at our driving range one day. The thing that struck me was the way he moved through the ball.

61

Fig 2.15 Clearing the left side a) Backswing b) Impact c) Finish
Good rotation of the hips will allow complete follow-through.

His left hip cleared beautifully every time. His body moved with the swing. There was no sensation of 'hit'. So the message is: 'Don't make the ball the focal point of your swing!'

You know when you have struck the ball well the moment after impact. You know that 'feeling', without ever having to look up. It feels almost as if you struck nothing,

a)

b)

as if there was no 'resistance' at impact. It's a wonderful feeling. The knack is to swing wide. So, do not make the ball the focal point of your *next* swing. Swing past it. Forget about your backswing. Give it a big follow-through.

Remember: The most important part of the swing happens after impact.

Fig 2.16 At impact, bad golfers will have their left hip facing the ball, while good golfers will have their mid-line facing the target.

c)

ST PETERSBURG

A golfer got to heaven and found it was full of great golf courses. One of them looked really tough. He was watching a golfer trying to strike a ball over an enormous lake onto a green 350 yards away.

'Who does he think he is — Jesus Christ?' asked the newcomer.

'That is Jesus Christ,' said a passing angel. 'His trouble is, he thinks he's Seve Ballesteros.'

CHOOSING THE CORRECT 'ANGLES'

A question! What is the most important thing in golf, and why? The answer — the angle of the clubface precisely as it strikes the ball at impact. A fact — it does not matter in which direction you swing in golf! If you swing left and your clubface is facing right (open to the swing-line), the ball will never end up left of target — it will always slice off to the right. It is not the direction that is important, but what angle your clubface is at as it collides with the static ball. I often tell pupils: 'The important thing is how you arrive, not how you drive!'

Fig 3.1 If you want the ball to travel towards the target, the clubface must be square as it strikes the ball.

▶ SHAPING YOUR SHOT

If you think golf is a difficult game, you will be convinced after this chapter! The real problem is that you can strike a ball in a certain direction but it may well not have the decency to stay there! Take for example the dreaded slice shot, where the ball finishes way right of the target (see Fig 3.2). This shot actually starts off left of the target. I often compare what happens in this shot to a boat going down a river. Your arms are like the power, the engine and the body of the boat. The rudder is the clubface. The smallest change in the angle of the rudder will have a huge bearing on the direction of the boat. Amazingly, the slightest change in the clubface angle at impact has a huge bearing on the flight of the ball. Unfortunately you will never witness this at impact as it happens so fast — too fast for the eye to behold. You will only see the resulting shot.

Fig 3.2 This open clubface will result in a slice.

The slice is probably the most common 'bad' shot in golf. It is always most frustrating. All that effort for a high, weak shot. I am always reminded of someone pouring water into a bucket with a big hole in it. The water (power) is escaping. The cause is an open clubface. The cure is to 'knuckle down' — show more knuckles on your left hand grip — the finger grip (see Fig 1.11). This may feel terribly uncomfortable at first but the result, if you are able to put up with it, will be dramatic because with this alteration in your grip you will present a closed position at impact. The balls will tend to go straight, or you may even hook them slightly to the left. So you must change your 'attitude' and stop anticipating the slice to the right. Attack the area where you are having the problem — go straight for it. Aim right if you are afraid of the right, do not anticipate the slice. If you succeed in swinging it out to the right, you have cured both your clubface angle and swing-line problems. Remember, it only works because of the awkwardness!

I will let you in on a trade secret: when afflicted with the open (or closed for that matter) clubface at impact, never try to move directly to the square position. Always try to exaggerate the cure. Go from open to trying to close the face. If you are lucky, the clubface will return square at impact. I always say there is some excuse for hitting a different type of bad shot in golf, but there is no excuse for striking the same old tired slice or hook shot again and again. If you cannot shape your shots, you haven't got what I call 'a handle on the game'. You do not understand the importance of your clubface angles as you address the ball, throughout the entire swing and most especially at impact. Your clubface angle at impact determines how you play!

Golf is all about ball control. A good tip is to hold the clubface angle square to the flag as you strike the ball. This works even on putts — hold the putter head square to the hole as you strike the putt, marry one to the other.

(See the typical 'golf lesson' on correcting the slice in the Appendix: Lesson 1.)

▶ THE ANGLES

There are three angles the clubface can take at impact: square, open, and closed (see Figs 3.3, 3.4, 3.5). The clubface can hold one of these three positions throughout the entire swing.

Fig 3.3 Square clubface

Fig 3.4 Open clubface

Fig 3.5 Closed clubface

If a golfer presents the *closed* clubface at the top of his backswing, I know immediately that he will hook or pull left, and the ball will end up left of the target. His shots will lack height and he will have desperate trouble chipping around the green. His Driver will also be rested for some time! (The Driver face has an 11 degree loft: if even slightly closed at impact the ball will never get airborne.) These type of shots have a lot of top-spin on them when the ball hits the ground and they generally create more distance.

If you strike with an *open* clubface (the clubface pointing right of the target), the ball will end up right of target. Shots with an open clubface will also be very high and lack distance. Much of the force of your swing is lost through the open clubface. The open clubhead creates back-spin so that the shots lack distance and tend to kick sideways on landing.

If you strike the ball with the clubface *squarely* on target, your shot will be on target.

Generally speaking, golfers who play with the closed face are very bad players around the green. Their short game is appalling while their long game may be adequate. When a golfer says: 'I have a good long game but a poor short game', I suspect that a closed clubface at impact is responsible.
Alternatively, if he/she suffers from a poor long game and a good short game, the problem is an open face at impact.

Fig 3.6 If the hands are positioned as shown, it will inevitably lead to a closed clubface at impact.

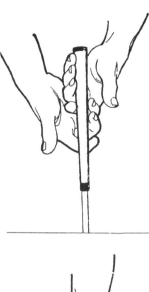

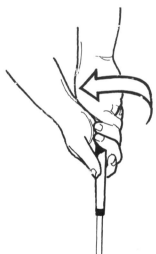

THE GRIP GAUGE

A tense grip is a disaster in golf!

What you do at one end of the club has a huge bearing on the other end. Your grip has a huge bearing on the clubface angle. Amazingly, golfers who slice and hook the ball are always trying to correct the fault by swing alterations. They may feel a fault in the strike and may well hit a very bad shot. While this is caused in part by a bad swing, the faulty impact originated further back than the swing — it was in the actual grip. Top-class players always change the flight pattern by altering the grip position, rarely ever changing their swing. The altered grip position effects the flight changes for them. Bad golf/good golf — flight changes start in the grip.

You must learn to operate the 'grip gauge'. Here's how it works. Your hands and arms have a natural, neutral position (a set angle) when they are hanging from the body. Once you move your hands out of this natural, normal position, they will want to revert immediately back to normality (to the original angle).

Strong grip

For example, if I place my two hands as shown in Fig 3.6 they will feel uncomfortable, and the very first chance they get they will revert back to the neutral position (try this out for yourself). In other words during the backswing they will turn back towards normality and so close the clubface, thus presenting a closed position at impact (see Fig 3.5). The ball will definitely lack height and will go leftwards. Short-game problems are a certainty. I call this right-hand position 'fisting it' — right hand grip is in the palm and much too tight.

Weak grip

Similarly, if I position my left hand as shown in Fig 3.7 during the swing, it rotates back and opens the face, resulting in the inevitable slice (see Fig 3.2). I will always remember a 'knowledgeable' man who told me he had a hook problem for twenty years. He was forever trying to correct his swing.

Fig 3.7 The 'V' on the left hand, pointing towards the left shoulder, signifies a weak grip and a resulting open clubface.

He felt it too humiliating to admit that the actual problem was in his grip! I must make one very important point here: there is no such thing as *the* perfect grip (there is, however, such a thing as a bad grip), but there is *one* perfect grip for you. I call this the 'grip gauge'. Your barometer must be the flight of the ball on your shots.

▶ SQUARE AT IMPACT PLEASE!

An amazing fact is that the clubface only needs to be square *precisely as it hits the ball*. Many golfers are under two misconceptions, the first being that you must swing the club straight back and straight through. This is actually impossible because what results is a steep swing. As your arms are attached to your shoulders, if you try to swing straight back, the club will inevitably go outside, very steep, and you will always come 'across' the ball. The second misconception is that you must hold the clubface square for the duration of the swing. This is another impossibility and has disastrous consequences. What happens? The clubface closes on the backswing and is very closed at impact — shots hook, or even pull-hook, left.

So what happens in the actual golf swing? The clubface is square as you start. What you hope for is that you will return to square at impact, but by turning the body, the 'L' turn, the clubface is in the half-way position. This appears to be an open position, but the clubface is actually square to the body. As you will see in Fig 3.10, at the top of the backswing the clubface can be in three positions: a closed position (A) whereby shots will be left and lacking height; an open position (B) which will result in a slice, and the square position — the correct angle (C).

3.8

3.9

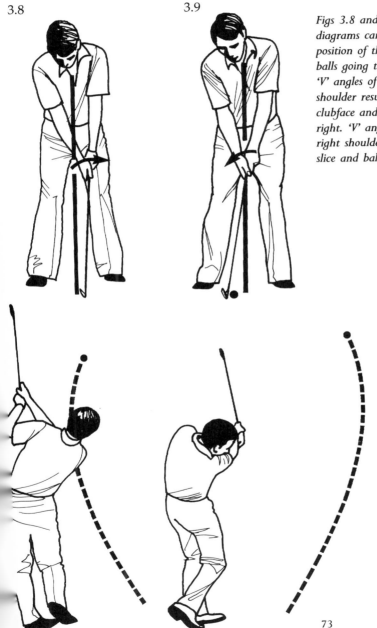

Figs 3.8 and 3.9 Study these diagrams carefully. Note the position of the hands for balls going to right and left. 'V' angles of hands to left shoulder results in open clubface and ball swings to right. 'V' angles of hands to right shoulder corrects the slice and ball swings to left.

Fig 3.10 Clubface angles at top of backswing will determine the impact positions.

a) Shut clubface — a certain hook
b) Open clubface — a sure slice
c) Square at top — correct angle

IT'S A MARRIAGE!

If the clubface is open to the swing-line, or closed, you are going to get swerve on the shot, and this could result in a pull to the left or a push to the right. If you can get the direction of your swing towards the target and your clubface square to that, all will go on line.

▶ SUMMARY

'Slice right — knuckle down'

If your shots are 'high' and 'right', you should position your hands more to the right of the grip. As you move your hands away from their normal position, they will work their way back during the swing and present a slightly closed face at impact. (See Fig 3.9.)

'Leftward shots — Hooks — No knuckles'

If your shots are flying 'left' and 'low', operate the grip gauge in a different manner. Move your hands to the left. Weaken your grip. Your hands will tend to work their way back to normality and open out the clubface at impact. (See Fig 3.8.)

You must have the determination and concentration to work on your grip — find a grip gauge angle that works for *you*.

a)

b)

A GRIPPING STORY!

John McDermott had the worst slice in the club. One day he surpassed himself with his slice. The golf course ran anti-clockwise (traditional) and all the trouble was on the right-hand side — the slicer's nightmare. He sliced the fifth tee off, sixth, seventh, eighth. At the ninth he teed up the ball and aimed away to the left in order to prevent the shot going right. He struck the ball very hard and it sailed right over the wall on the right-hand side, hit a car windscreen and shattered it. The car collided with a van, almost killing the unfortunate driver. After giving details to the police, John carried on. Having lost nine more golf-balls, he headed for the eighteenth hole. He shot the ball right through the professional's shop window! Both the secretary and the professional stormed over to John. 'What are you going to do about it?' screamed the professional. 'I think,' said John, 'if I move my left hand a little more over the shaft....'

POWER WITHOUT EFFORT

LEVERAGE AND POWER

As a golfer you must understand the meaning of the word 'leverage'. If you apply 'leverage' to your swing you may succeed in driving the ball enormous distances.

Have you ever thought why it is that great players who swing slowly can still drive the ball enormous distances? Or have you ever tried to strike a ball short of a drain, swung very easily at it, but the ball flew into the drain, leaving you to think, 'I should have tried to get over it in the first place.' Remember, you only have to strike the golf ball ONCE! So you only need power *once* in your swing.

Fig 4.1 This diagram shows the power going through the shaft and flexing close to the clubhead.

To achieve maximum distance with a minimum of effort you must learn about the part leverage plays in the swing, and realise above all that the projectile (the ball) is only 1.68 inches (4.26cm) in diameter and 1.62 ounces (45.92g) in weight. Therefore, it is not massive power you need, rather *precise* power. The great players manage to disguise their use of power very well — they are very discreet about it.

Where do you need power in a golf swing? You need it in the clubhead. And when do you need it? You need it precisely at impact. I often say to pupils: 'Do you know you only have to strike the ball once. Save your power for that moment.' Think of how you use a hammer — you activate the head. Alternatively, in fishing you cast by putting the bend on the outer extremity of the rod — the clubhead is the outer extremity of the golf club.

The secret of power is 'opposing forces'. Power is never created, it is released! Think of a wall and a spring. You press the spring against the wall, then you take your hand away and release the spring. The secret of power has to do with resistance. The wall is resisting the action of the spring, and by taking your hand away and releasing the spring, power is released. It is the same in golf: you don't try to create power, you don't try to force the shot, you have got to allow power to be released. The real secret is that you must be able to put your body in all the unusual positions, that is, awkward ones that it will want to get out of. Now, if

you are able to organise the collision and

then the escape back to normality in a way that will create power on-plane, you have found real power and have solved the mystery of distance.

A word of warning! Your body is like water rolling down the side of a mountain — it will always take the easiest point of relief. Your body will resist this collision if it can at all.

(See the typical 'golf lesson' on how to improve your distance in the Appendix: Lesson 2.)

POWER BASES

In the great golf swing minor explosions take place. What top-class players do is create a number of power bases. Let me explain. You create all your swing power swinging back, and you release it going forwards. You must never try to create swing power on your forward swing, speeding up as you come into the ball. You release power.

Power base 1 — your back

Your knees are the foundation, the resistance, the wall. When you address a ball and start your backswing, you should start a collision. How does it work? Your legs are the resistance and your top half is turning. One part of your body is turning in a certain direction and the other part is staying still — resisting (see Fig 4.2). You have created a collision and you will have power 'stored' in your back at the top of your backswing. A lot of golfers turn their shoulders when they swing back, but they

Fig 4.2 Check your 'turn' by
studying your shadow. Check
that you are not swaying
and that your back is to the
target.

also turn their legs and knees — everything
moves back. There is no resistance, therefore
there is no power created.

Think of the spring and the wall again. The
top half of your body turns against the
resistance of your knees. This is a very
unusual position for you, and your body
wants to get back to normality as fast as
possible. It is up to you to transfer the
power which you have in your back and get
it to register in the clubhead through impact.
If you can organise the escape back into
normality in a way that will help you to
power the ball, you have succeeded in the
Base 1 power situation.

Power base 2 — wrist cock

The greatest possible angle of resistance for the shaft is to place it directly against the left arm and use the resistance in the arms to create the collision. This is where you must learn to 'pump the power into your swing'.

Fig 4.3 You have achieved the ideal 'cocked' position when you see wrinkles on the back of your left wrist as it is turned towards your body.

Base 2 concerns your hands and arms and this is referred to in golf as the 'wrist cock'. Look at Fig 4.3. By pulling the hands and wrists back against the forearms the golfer has created a very unusual position for them and, naturally, they will want to get back to normality. The hands and wrists must be cocked against the resistance of the left arm. If your left arm collapses at the top of your swing, your wrist cock is useless. When I say cock your wrists, I don't mean break your elbow!

If I swing back, remembering to resist with my knees, turning my body, turning my 'L', when I am half way back I suddenly begin to cock my wrists and get into the position shown in Fig 4.3. As I swing back down towards the ball, down on the inside, my hands kick back to normality — wrist

81

Fig 4.4 Your 'power kick'
will release the clubhead.

uncocking — and I have second power base (see Fig 4.4). To explain this further, most golfers fail to release the clubhead — they strike with the handle of the club (see Fig 2.5). What they end up with is a swing where the clubhead is locked into the arms. This means that the clubhead's speed is totally limited to the arm speed. The great players are not happy with this; they have what I call the 'power kick' in their swing. They 'power kick' the clubhead by releasing it and getting it to fly past their hands through the hitting area (see Fig 4.4). This is done by virtue of the 'wrist cock' and the subsequent release of the clubhead. Another way of looking at this is to look at the shaft angle in relation to the left arm. Narrow this angle as shown in Fig 4.5 — now widen it again. Narrow, Widen.

Fig 4.5 Check your arms for the triangular positions. Straighten your arm early on in the downswing.

Most golfers get into the wrong position in the top of the backswing — they lock the swing at the top (see Fig 4.6). The ideal position at the top of your backswing is where the shaft of your club is on-line towards the target, the clubface is square and your wrists are cocked. You might ask

'Why do you need the shaft on-line?'. Well, if your shaft is off-line, you will never swing towards the target (on-line). If your clubface is open or closed at the top, it will be open or closed at impact. If your wrists are not cocked you will never release. You may ask: 'How will I ever think of all these things at the top of the swing and still manage to hit the ball?' I am going to let you in on another little secret — if you get one right the others will automatically follow. If you are able to get your hands into the 'wrist cock' position, underneath the shaft, the clubface will automatically be square and the shaft on-line at the top. Therefore you will swing towards the target and the clubface will be square to your swing-line. I sometimes say to pupils: 'You never knew how handy your right ear could be.' They ask me what I mean. I reply: 'You aim the shaft towards it at the top of your swing. If you use your right ear as a marker, the shaft will automatically be on-line. (See Fig 4.3.)

The correct position is so important in the backswing. If I were to instruct the greatest player in the world to adopt the *wrong* position at the top of his backswing, he would never break 80.

Fig 4.6 At the top of the backswing the shaft should point in the direction of the target. In this diagram the dotted line is showing the correct direction of the shaft.

▶ POWER RELEASE

Stay behind the ball with your upper body, but lever the clubhead forward at the same time. As you are swinging towards the ball, the power that you create in your back, and by cocking your wrists, is all travelling in the direction of the ball. This power is travelling on a very high level and the ball is very low. Unfortunately most golfers never succeed in transferring the power they have created down to the clubhead. Think of it like this: there are two things travelling towards the ball — your hands and upper body and your clubhead. Your hands are on the inner extremity and the clubhead is on the outer extremity. Your hands only have to travel three feet (1m) while your clubhead has to travel nine feet (3m). Imagine you are driving along a dual carriageway, you decide you want to pass out a car that is on your inside but suddenly the car speeds up and you will never pass it. Think of another situation. You are driving along the carriageway, you want to pass out this car, suddenly it stops and you shoot by. This is what the great players do. One astonishing result of a study found that the top half of great golfers' bodies moves back as they are hitting the ball. In contrast, when most high handicap golfers are coming in for their shot, they suddenly think, 'I'll give it a little bit more, I'll try to hit it a bit harder'; they move their upper body forward to help with the hit.

A golf club is a machine. The secret is to get the power down to the clubhead. The point is, if the clubhead must move forwards, the handle and the top half of the body must move back. If you could imagine that as you are hitting a golf-ball somebody gets a hook, hooks your hand back through the hitting area and allows the clubhead to come forward to strike the ball for you. The secret of golf is that you have to learn not to hit the ball, not to 'become personally involved' — allow the clubhead to hit it for you. I call this 'learning to keep your hands at home'. (See Fig 4.4.)

Fig 4.7 Your swing must focus on the clubhead and not on the handle of the club.

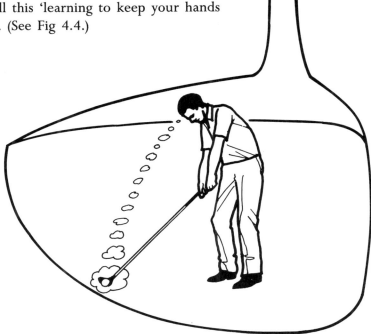

here are only two parts to a golf swing.)ne is that you create power, the other is ๅat you release it. The difference between ๅe great player and the trier is that the trier ever gets to release the power. I refer to ๅis as the 'deflective theory' — you have to ⁞ able to deflect the power away from the ⸱dy and bounce it down to the clubhead. It 'ghostly power' that you need around the ⸱ll!

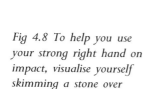

► DRILLS

There are exercises that will help you enormously. One involves learning to bend the bottom of the shaft of the club — as you strike, bend the shaft on the ball at impact (see Fig 4.1). This is a tremendous exercise for strengthening your hands and wrists.

Fig 4.8 To help you use your strong right hand on impact, visualise yourself skimming a stone over water.

Another good exercise focuses on the lower half of the club and on the clubhead. Go into rough grass and start to clip the clubhead through the grass. Visualise skimming a stone over water. Use your strong right hand at impact. Hit it once during your swing with your right hand (see Fig 4.8).

Anybody can put power into the shaft of a golf club, but it takes a great golfer to put the power into the head of the club. The real power in golf comes from the right forearm, into the clubhead and through the hitting area. You release the clubhead using the power of the right forearm. If you can manage to turn the 'L' and a slight wrist cock, swing down on the inside and stay behind with the top half of your body, and 'power kick' the clubhead with your right forearm through the ball, you will have a tremendous golf swing. The power you need in golf is not power in the body or power from the body, rather power down to the clubhead.

In the middle of every good golf swing there should be a 'chip'. Think of what you do when you chip a ball — you flick it up into the air. It is the very same chipping action you should include in your swing. Work the hands well. Start with an 8 Iron and spend some time hitting short 'chip' shots (think of leverage!). Now, with the Driver try to retain this 'chipping' feel as you strike the ball.

Fig 4.9 Anybody can put power into the shaft of a golf club, but it takes a great golfer to put the power into the head of the club.

▶ SUMMARY

I have talked about the slow tempo of the great players, yet the enormous distances they manage to drive the ball — I call this the 'slow fast swing' or 'stiff wristy swing'. Slow body swing — fast clubhead. It reminds me of the perfect swimmer, the duck — so graceful, gliding along over the water, hardly causing a ripple. Nothing much seems to be happening, yet the webbed feet are very active under the water. It is the same in the good golf swing — the great players are very discreet with their power. Their upper body remains very steady at impact (economy of movement), but they are working the

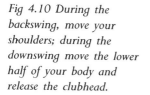

Fig 4.10 During the backswing, move your shoulders; during the downswing move the lower half of your body and release the clubhead.

clubhead very hard. When you notice them grimace at impact, you must understand that they are trying very hard to hold their body in position (back) while they bend the clubhead end on the ball. The slow body and the activated clubhead. The clubhead, like the webbed feet, is the accelerator of the ball — and they know it!

We all have basic power. We can lift a chair, push a car, chop a log. Can we use this power in golf? Power is created by turning the top half against the resisting lower half going back, and by the wrist cock, and resisting the impulse to lunge forward on the forward swing, rather to release the lower half and the clubhead. Think of an elevator — the power is stored on the second floor of your backswing. However, you must drop it all down to the first floor if you are to benefit from it at impact. Most golfers spend their time fooling around on the wrong floor! They lunge their upper body forward at impact and hit with the handle of the club. It's upstairs going back and downstairs on the forward swing.

SON OF A ....
Father Murphy, the new curate, was encouraged to join the local golf club. He was a terrible golfer. Members quickly found out and avoided him.

One Saturday he was lucky enough to find a new member who agreed to play with him. The newcomer suggested they put a decent wager on the game. The priest fancied his chances as the newcomer scraped the first hole.

Once the money went on, however, all changed. Suddenly the newcomer played like a man possessed. He beat Fr Murphy and won the five pounds wager.

'Tell me,' said Fr Murphy, 'do your parents live in the parish?'

'Yes,' replied the newcomer, slightly puzzled. 'Why, would you like to meet them for a game?'

'No,' said Fr Murphy, 'a thought occurred to me. If you brought them round to the church one day, I'd marry them!'

READING BALL FLIGHT

5

GETTING A 'HANDLE' ON YOUR GAME

Have you ever wondered why one day you play well and think you have it, then you go out the next day and play the most awful golf? Or you play a storming front nine and then your game collapses. Why? Simply because you do not have a handle on the game. When you are on your own the teaching pro is the golf ball. It never lies. The ball in the air draws a picture of your swing on the ground. A teaching pro I once knew used to insist on turning his back on his pupils, observing only the ball flight and taking the directions solely from it. I have always thought there is some excuse for striking a different type of bad shot, but none for repeating the same one. Your attitude must be to never ever say 'What did I do wrong in the swing?', rather to ask 'What does the little ball tell me?' The reason this is important is because golf is a game of opposites. Ben Hogan once remarked: 'If you do the opposite to every natural instinct you have, you will come near the perfect swing.' There is nothing logical about golf and we are instinctively set up wrong for it. When things begin to go wrong with our shots, we become frustrated and end up taking all the wrong options. For example, if you swing leftwards the ball will most likely go to the right. And in order to save the shot you will try to hit the ball even more to the left. This will of course have the opposite effect. Similarly, if you swing down on the ball, the most likely result will be the 'sky' shot. If you swing very hard and force the shot, you will put all the force into the handle of the club and probably lose distance, as no power is getting down to the clubhead.

▶ BALL FLIGHT

The earliest golf-balls were made from wood. There was a major breakthrough in 1848 with the gutta percha ball, which was filled with a rubber-like substance. Initially this had a smooth surface and tended to go up and come down very quickly. It was found that after some time — when it became damaged through use — the ball began to hang in the air for longer, and thus the idea of markings on the face of the ball (indentations) came

Fig 5.1 You must learn to 'read' the ball flight if you want to correct your game.

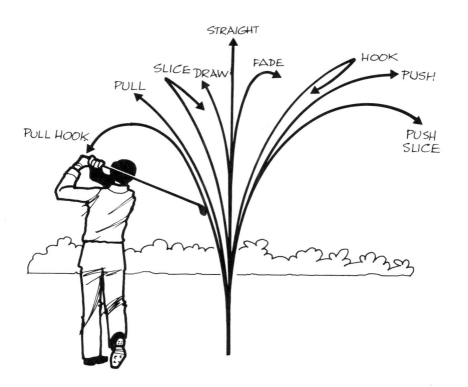

about. The modern ball with its dimple effect stays airborne for much longer. However, with this added advantage comes serious problems.

Spin and swerve

Consider the flight of a golf shot from beginning to end: a) the ball can start out in the direction of the target, or left or right of it, b) it can go very high, reasonably high, or low, c) it can swerve left or right at the end of the flight, or it can hit the target. The direction the ball takes off in is a result of what is called the *swing-line,* the direction your arms are going in, and the force of the shot will dominate the early part of the flight. Now, as the force begins to die off, whatever direction that golf-ball is spinning in (this is the result of the *clubface angle* at impact), that is going to be the major factor. The point here is very simple. You may well swing left but the clubface angle could be pointing right at impact, so that even though you may drive the ball leftwards, it might be 'spinning' towards the right. As the force begins to die, the spin takes over. In the slice shot, probably the most common shot in golf, the ball starts out to the left and wickedly veers to the right towards the end. What has happened here is that the golfer has swung across the ball to the left with an open clubface. He has driven the ball leftwards and, even though it initially travels leftwards, it is spinning towards the right and will, as the force begins to die away, veer round towards the right at the end of the flight. To repeat what has happened: his arms have swung leftwards, but his clubface was actually pointing to the right at impact.

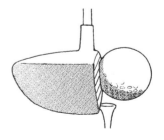

Similarly, a shot which hooks left is caused by a clubface angle that is closed to the actual line of the swing at impact.

▶ HEIGHT

The height on your golf shots is determined by the part of the ball that is struck, that is, the top, middle or bottom (see Figs 1.8 and 1.9). This is referred to as the angle of attack, the *plane* of the swing. If you hit the bottom of the ball, the club will inflict a lot of back-spin and the shot will have a high flight. Therefore, if your shots tend to go too high, your swing-plane is too steep and you are coming down on the ball. The top of the clubhead is contacting the bottom of the ball, thus creating excessive back-spin — creating a high, if not an actual 'sky' shot.

The important factor here isn't really what direction the ball starts off in, rather it is where the ball ends up! So spin is one of the big, big factors in golf. And to drive the point home, spin is caused by an open or closed clubface at impact.

▶ LEARN TO 'LEFT-SPIN' THE BALL

The type of spin the great golfers inflict on the golf-ball is called a left-spin. It is the same as a conversion in rugby or soccer: when the player hits the ball, he drives it up into the air, swinging his leg from right to left, from inside to outside. And as the ball is in the air, it has slight left-spin, even though it is driven forwards and it is going to curve 'gently' towards the left at the end of the flight. This is the ideal flight for a maximum distance shot because the angle of attack will always be shallow — direct. If you are an habitual slicer the ball is going to be travelling (spinning) towards the right at the end. To inflict this type of spin you have to *swing* the club across the ball from the outside, and inevitably it will be a steeper swing and lack the penetration of the other swing. The force of the swing is going to go into the ground — downwards. If your shots are lacking distance and much too *high,* you are chopping the ball, your swing-plane is too *steep.*

AVOID THE BAD, BAD SHOTS!

There are what I call bad shots in golf, and there are bad, bad shots. There are two families of bad shots, one much worse than the other. If you are in the 'out to in' category of swinger, where you come at the ball from the outside, there are a possible six bad shots you can get (See chapter 2, page 51). The interesting thing here is that shots which seem to be quite different have a similar background. They could be called blood brothers. For example, you could set up on a tee, hit the ball from left to right and slice it. In other words, the ball ends up on the right-hand side of the fairway or in the rough. On the next tee you could make the same swing and the ball could go straight left (pull). The two shots seem totally different but they are in fact very similar. The slice is caused by an 'out to in' swing, swinging leftwards, and the clubface is open to the swing-line (slice right), but the second time the clubface is square to the swing-line (pull left) and the ball flies to the left. This can be very, very confusing. You may think there are two different swings involved here, but it really is just one factor that has changed — the angle of the clubface.

BE AWARE OF LOFT ANGLE

An even more extraordinary thing is that you can have the same swing and the same angle and get different results by using different types of clubs. You can get a different shape on the club. For example, with the 3 Iron you can swing across the ball with an open clubface, getting a vicious slice, and then do exactly the same swing with your 8 Iron and the ball goes miles left (see Fig 5.2). Why is this? It is because the loft angle has a huge bearing on the spin of

Fig 5.2 If you were to use different lofted clubs and exactly the same swing for all, the flight patterns would inevitably be different, for example, the No 1 Driver could slice and the No 3 Wood could give a straighter shot.

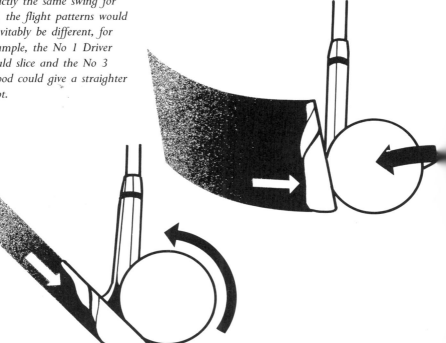

the golf-ball. With the 8 Iron, because of the angle on the face, it is the bottom of the face that strikes the bottom of the ball, and even if the face is slightly open it will always cause back-spin, so the ball will always go on a straight line. In contrast, with the 3 Iron and an open face, it's the middle of the face hitting the middle of the ball which will always give you right-spin. Where you have the same swing and the same clubface angle, by virtue of using different lofted clubs you will get huge variance in the flight patterns. You could hit your 3 Wood fairly straight because the angle on the Wood is more forgiving — the bottom of the face will contact the bottom half of the ball and create more back-spin. Try the same with the Driver and it will shoot viciously to the right. The 3 Wood is hiding a fault in your swing whereas the Driver is showing you that the clubface is slightly open to your swing-line. When someone says 'I'm hooking my Wedge and slicing my Driver', their swing has not changed at all.

So, if you wanted to find out whether you had an open or a closed clubface, or if your clubface was 'misbehaving', your low Irons would tell you. If you wanted to find out about your swing-line, your lofted 8s and 9s would tell you. The secret is to be able to accurately describe the shots you hit and then to define them. There are the bad, bad shots — the slice and the pull, the shank, sky, fluff and pull-hook. They represent one family of shots. For example, if you swing across from the outside and you slice the ball, you are also very likely to pull the ball to the left and get the odd sky shot. Now, if

Fig 5.3 Position of ball in (A) shows 'shank' impact; position of ball in (B) shows 'pull' impact.

a)

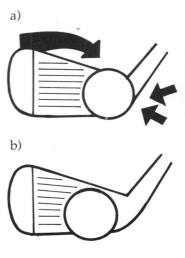

b)

97

you pull the ball with your arms to the left, it means you are coming across the ball from the outside and the ball is going to be hit quite near the shank of the club. Golfers who suffer from the 'shank shot' are original pullers of the ball, so the different varieties of shots are all coming from the same type of swing (see Fig 5.3). If you can get at the ball from the other angle, from the inside, and get your attack from inside to outside (as the soccer player does), there is a possibility that you can push the ball or hook it, or even push-slice it, but you cannot slice, pull or sky the ball from these positions (see Fig 5.4).

Fig 5.4 An 'out to in' swing (A) will give you six bad shots; an 'in to out' swing (B) will give a possible three bad shots.

a)

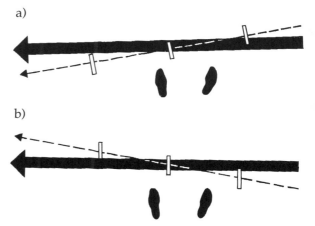

b)

▶ VARY YOUR PRACTICE

I was watching a champion golfer train during the winter. He came to the driving range night after night. I was amazed at his patience when practising. All around him golfers were 'slugging' the ball. In the three months I watched him practise, he never hit a full shot. He concentrated on punches, high fades, finesse shots all the time. This should be a lesson to you: you must get away from the power syndrome. Shape your play, get a handle on that ball. Nominate the shot you are going to play. Slow everything down — don't compete with the golfer in the next bay. Pattern your play. Learn ball control.

If you want to become a really class player, place yourself behind a tree or some obstacle, take out a 7/8 Iron and try manoeuvring the golf-ball around the tree.

What I mean is, try to hit the ball from right to left, then hit it from left to right, or alternatively chip it over the tree.

is up to you to decide what shape of shot

you prefer. Try to get a pattern going and stick to it. The low handicap golfers like to 'draw' the ball with the long shots. You can certainly play golf with a controlled slice, but it's very unlikely that you will play off anything lower than a twelve handicap. If you can play the power fade or the power draw, you can play off anything you want really. If you want the maximum distance shot then you have got to learn to left-spin the ball.

▶ HOW TO SELF-CORRECT AND BREAK AWAY FROM MEDIOCRITY

Here are some sample analyses you should make at the range or on the practice ground. You hit the ball and it goes along the ground — by analysing the flight you will find that the ball was struck on the very top (see Fig 1.9). Rather than ask 'What did I do wrong in my swing?', you've got to say 'I must hit the bottom of the ball, I must get

Fig 5.5 Your grip will determine the clubface angle at impact.

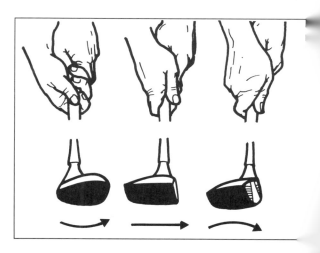

the clubhead to the other part of the ball'. If the ball goes way to the left, then you must ask 'Why did the ball go left and hook more left at the finish of the flight?' It was of course because the clubface was closed to your swing-line (see Fig 5.5). You must work on the clubface angle. The clubface angle is governed by your grip. Weaken your grip — no knuckles should be visible on your left hand — and fan the clubhead open as you start back. Rotate your left arm in order to do this on take-away. If you slice the ball, you must deduce that you inflicted right-spin on the ball, with an open clubface for a steep outside angle. To cure this, you must school yourself into presenting a closed clubface at impact — alter your grip once again and hood the clubface on take-away (that is, keep it looking at the ball).

Fig 5.6 Try to have the clubface to the ball 'ahead' of your hands.

▶ DISTANCE

If your shots are lacking distance, then you are not compressing the ball at impact, you lack clubhead speed, you don't understand leverage — you must learn to waggle the clubhead at address and unlock that swing of yours. Go for an excessive wrist cock and a very early release. Try to have the clubface to the ball before your hands. The legendary American golfer Sam Snead once said: 'Feel that your wrists are oily — strike hard with your strong hand' (that is, your right hand). Work the stick — let the clubhead go at the ball. Follow the clubhead to achieve maximum distance with minimum effort. You must never become personally involved — let the clubhead take over.

'Power kick' the clubhead forward rather than the body. It is very difficult to power kick the clubhead forward and at the same time hold the top half of your body back. This is what is demanded in successful golf — to learn not to strike, but to allow the clubhead to do it for you.

Golf starts from a 'dead ball' situation. *You* are responsible for inflicting every aspect of flight on this 'dead ball'. To become a class player, you must develop a swing that works for you and analyse your game so as to be able to accurately describe and name your shot patterns, and immediately change the shape of your shots if there is a problem.

Fig 5.7 is a summary of the game of golf. It breaks the flight of the ball into separate compartments and analyses right back through the swing. If you are able to see the various compartments, you will have jumped right into the tournament player's mind. The following notes will help you interpret the chart.

SECTION A *(Read chart downwards)*

This section summarises how height is determined by swing plane.

If you set up with a strong left side and a compressed right side, you will automatically turn better, which ensures a wide backswing. Take advantage of this by swinging in with a shallow (rather than steep) attack and drive the ball away at the perfect elevation. The perfect angle of elevation for a drive is 45 degrees — this is directly due to the part of the ball you strike and to the plane of your attack. The plane of your attack is determined by your set-up.

SECTION B *(Read across from Section A)*

This section summarises how direction is determined by clubface angle.

If your shots are to fly straight, then the ball must have back-spin (not excessive) and your clubface must be square (not open or closed) at impact. This is directly due to your grip angle at impact. Your grip controls the clubface angle, it determines the degree of spin on the flight, and this creates the swerve on the shot.

SECTION C *(Read across from Section B)*

This section summarises how clubhead speed determines distance.

Fig 5.7 THE ULTIMATE SHOT

Section A
SWING PLANE

1 → Start by setting up with a GOOD LEFT SIDE. . .

2 → Your swing must be a WIDE one . . .

3 → The force of your swing must be applied from BEHIND . . .

4 → The ball will be driven FORWARDS . . .

↓

PERFECT HEIGHT

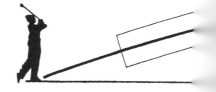

The distance a ball travels is directly due to clubhead speed at impact. Clubhead speed comes from a swing that has leverage. A swing with leverage comes from 'oily wrists' at address — you sense 'fluidity' and loosen up your swing.

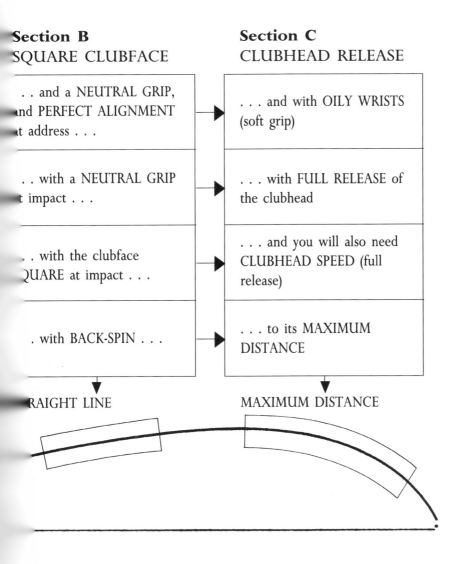

Section B SQUARE CLUBFACE	Section C CLUBHEAD RELEASE
. . and a NEUTRAL GRIP, nd PERFECT ALIGNMENT t address . . .	. . . and with OILY WRISTS (soft grip)
. . with a NEUTRAL GRIP t impact . . .	. . . with FULL RELEASE of the clubhead
. . with the clubface QUARE at impact . . .	. . . and you will also need CLUBHEAD SPEED (full release)
. with BACK-SPIN . . .	. . . to its MAXIMUM DISTANCE

RAIGHT LINE   MAXIMUM DISTANCE

GOLF MYSTERIES
REVEALED!
'Golf is such a mad, stupid,
infuriating, crazy game,'
says the weekend player.
'You know I'm glad I don't
have to play again until
next Sunday!'

THE SHORT GAME

MASTERING THE SHORT GAME

In the long game you need 'accuracy' and 'distance'. You need a wide sweeping swing with 'leverage'. In the short game you just need accuracy. I call the short game the 'money department'. This is where you are going to become a champion or fail. This is it!

Fig 6.1 The short game

The clubs numbered 6, 7, 8, 9 and 10 and the Sand Wedge are designed for shorter play. It may be difficult to drive like Seve Ballesteros or Nancy Lopez, but mastering the short game is an attainable goal. You should decide right now that you are going to improve an area that requires no force —

107

simply accuracy. Become a demon chipper and putter and win, win, win! You need accuracy and height.

A startling statistic is that 65 per cent of all the shots you play are within a thirty-yard (27m) radius of the green. Now we are all capable of striking the ball thirty yards, even on our worst day. The question is, can we strike the ball accurately to a specific target? It is a very attainable short-range goal.

These shots are mastered at the impact position where the clubface is square to the target precisely as it strikes the ball. What you must learn to do is to lock the clubhead to the target at impact, to magnetise one to the other. The clubface itself is like the barrel of a gun — you aim it, or like the front of your car — you face it in a certain direction and then you drive it.

Here is the sequence you must follow. Stand in a position where the ball is directly between you and the target and:

1. Aim the clubface at the target.

2. Aim your feet, hips and shoulders slightly left of the target — open to the target line.

3. Place the ball well back in your stance — this ensures a downward blow on the ball with the Iron and a square position with your shoulders. Now 'pinch' the ball — take a divot. A lot of people make the mistake of trying to scoop the ball. You have to hit down on the ball in the short game and let the loft of the club bring

the ball up. You need height and you will only achieve this by striking down on the ball (it's a game of opposites!). Once you do this, the ball will begin to pop up for you and sit down on the green, beside the flag.

Fig 6.2 (left) The clubhead is being lined up with the target at address.

Fig 6.3 (right) The follow-through, keeping the clubface square to the target.

4. Keep most of your weight on the forward foot. It must remain there for the duration of the swing. This prevents swaying — moving off the ball.

5. Above all, play with 'dead hands'. Take the small muscles — the hands and wrists — out of the swing. Keep your swing stiff and in one piece. Use a very short backswing and extend triangle to target. The short backswing ensures an acceleration through the swing, even over the short distance.

Fig 6.4 For Wedge shots you need a steep swing. Use a second ball during practice to ensure a steep, sharp attack on the ball.

Use the 'L' swing (modified of course). Strike it down on the ball using some of the 'V' swing, and keeping the back of your left hand and the clubhead locked onto the target.

When a golfer complains about the short game, I immediately suspect his/her grip. You need a 'gentle touch' close to the green. Compare it to playing a piano — you play with your fingertips, never with the palms of your hands. Your right-hand grip is all about 'delicacy' and 'feel'. You don't strike the ball — you 'finesse' it. If you 'fist' (palm) the right-hand grip — forget it. Look at Fig 3.6. The right hand is out of its normal position; it will automatically revert back to its normal position and close the clubface at impact, thus preventing the essential height on the shot. A hooker's grip is simply disastrous for the short game. Players who are inflicted with this type of grip have to resort to a kind of scooping action around the green.

▶ PRACTICE ROUTINES

1. Straightforward pitch shot. Back of left hand to the flag

A good way to practise this shot is to get an umbrella, open it out and put it into the ground, twenty yards or so (18m) away from you. Pitch the ball into the brolly and work your way out gradually to longer shots. The secret here is to work out your alignment. You can do this by placing two clubs on the ground, one pointing directly towards the target, the other club slightly open to that line (left). Place the clubhead between the two clubs and then swing, making sure you hit down on the ball, getting the necessary height on it and getting the feeling of locking the clubhead to the target precisely at impact. As you move out from the umbrella, you progress up the shaft of the club and you lengthen your backswing slightly. A general rule of thumb — try to make the length of your forward swing twice that of your backswing. Get the feeling of a controlled backswing, and that you are hitting down and through the ball. If you use a very long backswing when you only need to drive the ball a very short distance, you will inevitably have a decelerating hit through the ball, usually resulting in a 'fluff' shot. I always remember working at a club which had a Par 5 in front of the shop. Golfers would hit two good wooden shots up near the green. They would take a driver-like backswing (complete overswing) for this thirty-yard (27m) shot and stick the club in the ground. My advice to someone with such a huge overswing would be: it's a swing I want, not an event. You have got to get a shorter backswing. You must realise that a shorter backswing allows for an accelerating forward swing even over a very short distance. You must attack the chip. Hit it down and through. In other words, don't be afraid to accelerate the clubhead through the ball. Short, back, down and through. If you cannot play this shot, you cannot play golf!

Fig 6.5 For the straightforward pitch shot, play the ball back in your stance and swing the back of your left hand towards the flag.

2. 'Cut up' shot. Extreme height on flight of ball over a short distance

This is what I call 'a must shot' — a shot where there is no other alternative. You are confronted with a bunker in your direct line to the pin, or some other similar type of hazard. The type of shot you must pull off is a very high one over a short distance and one that will 'sit down' quickly on the green. You must develop a technique of holding the clubface open as you slide it underneath the ball and finish with the clubface facing skywards (open) at the end of the swing. Don't close it!

Here is how it works (see Figs 6.6, 6.7, 6.8):

Fig 6.6 (left) Cut-up shot: use 'open' stance and aim clubface at target.

Fig 6.7 (centre) Swing 'out to in' along the feet line.

Fig 6.8 (right) Swing from outside 'across' the ball through impact, holding the clubface open.

- Aim your feet, hips and shoulders left of target (open stance). Aim the clubface at the target (clubface will be laid open). Play the ball opposite your left foot (forward in your stance).

- Using your right hand swing the club up very steeply. A definite 'V' type swing, and slightly outside going back, fanning the clubface open at the same time.

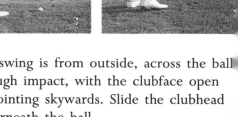

- The swing is from outside, across the ball through impact, with the clubface open or pointing skywards. Slide the clubhead underneath the ball.

It is a brilliant shot, but a very difficult one. It is interesting to note that even though the Sand Wedge face is very open at impact — it is the bottom edge (which is forward) that will strike the bottom of the ball — the ball will not fly right as with the Driver or Iron, but straight up, in a straight line.

You must aim your feet very much left of target, but aim the clubface directly at the target. Open it out. It is an 'all or nothing' shot. If you are going to play the shot, you must not 'chicken out' of it. Make sure you hit down and through the ball, following through to the end. Confidence is the key factor here. Convince yourself that you can play the shot, that you are good around the greens, that this is one of your better shots. Just before you commence your swing, lighten your grip, soften it, and swing longer and slower than you normally do. Make sure you do not stop at the ball. Swing right through it. Full follow-through.

THE BUNKER

The bunker is probably the area most feared by beginner golfers and a lot of handicap golfers. Your swing here must be 'out to in' with an open face. You 'slice' the ball out of the sand. The Sand Wedge is a club apart from the rest. It was designed specifically for the sand shot. Gene Sarazen, a legendary American golfer, told of how in 1933, while taking flying lessons, he pulled the control stick back, and as a consequence the tail-flaps went down and the nose simultaneously moved upwards. He related these actions to the principle of sand play. If the trailing edge of the Sand Wedge were lower than the leading edge, the club would cut through the sand more effectively, allowing for an explosion shot without the digging action of the conventional niblick. This is how the Sand Wedge was born. Forty-one years later, at the 126-yard (115m) eighth hole, known as the postage stamp, on Troon Golf Course, while playing in the 1973 British Open Championship, Gene Sarazen holed out his tee shot. Remarkable!

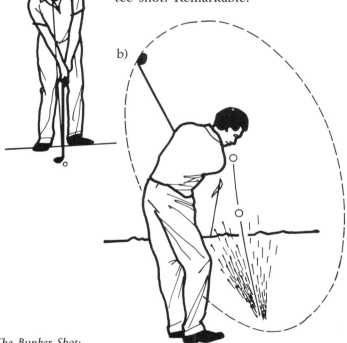

Fig 6.9 The Bunker Shot: the 'explosion' shot from the sand 'out to in', with the clubface open.

▶ **THE BUNKER SHOT**

It is important to realise that sand, being loose in texture, will react differently from soil. (See Fig 6.10) The main problem with bunker shots is when the clubface closes, so allowing the sand to accumulate in front of it, causing a 'fluffed shot'. Remember, the Sand Wedge was never meant to be used as

a bulldozer.

The same technique applies to the sand shot as to the cut-up shot we have just described. You aim your feet, hips and shoulders left of the target. (See Fig 6.6.) You aim the clubhead at the target. In order to do this, the clubhead must be laid wide open. (See Fig 6.9(a).) You should aim the clubhead about two inches (5cm) behind the ball. The swing must be 'out to in' or across the ball, keeping the face open or pointing skywards all the time. Try to get the feeling of keeping your body very, very steady as you strike and of sliding the clubhead underneath the ball rather than against it. Imagine there is an insect under the ball holding it up and you are going to cut the legs from under him (see Fig 6.9(b)). Handicap players are often tempted to look at the outcome of the shot before it is actually completed.

Fig 6.10 Use your feet as 'educators' in the sand. If the sand is hard the ball flies out; if the sand is loose the ball will come out slowly.

Where bunker shots are concerned, the need to keep the head still throughout the exercise cannot be overstated. Remember, once you hit the golf-ball it is history. You just have to wait for the result. The exercise of exploding a ball out of sand demands considerably more power than the inexperienced player might imagine. Beginners have a tendency to consider only the relatively short distance the ball may be required to travel from a green-side trap. Because of the high resistance, however, a full shot is absolutely vital. Use the explosion technique. The explosion shot should be played with the same tempo as that required to extract a ball from heavy rough.

The steep bunker shot

The situation will arise where you have a very steep bunker and a very short distance

115

to go. In this situation you should open the clubface even more, take the club up much quicker (steeper) and, keeping the clubface open, slide it underneath the ball — what I would call a severe version of the 'V' swing. You just pop it out!

The long bunker shot

The long bunker shot is the most difficult shot in golf. This is a speciality shot. The secret here is to school yourself into 'plucking' the ball from the sand. In other words, don't muck around with the sand. Get this ball out as clean as a whistle. Visualise the impact position. You have to feel that you are 'half' blading the ball — aim at the middle of the ball and get the feeling that, at impact, you are keeping your hands back and you are letting the clubhead go past your hands. It is very important to take a sufficiently lofted club, one that will ensure that the ball will clear the edge of the bunker. This shot requires plenty of practice.

Ball buried in sand

Occasionally you will be confronted with a ball that is buried in the sand. In this instance you have to reverse the technique adopted for the other shots: you must close the clubface and just swing the club back, bringing it down on top of the ball, keeping the face closed, with no follow-through whatsoever, and the ball will come out. When it hits the green, it will have quite an amount of top-spin on it. This shot is used to get the ball out of the bunker — it does not allow you to aim directly at the hole.

Fig 6.11 (above) Ball buried in the sand — a poached egg.

Fig 6.12 Close the clubface at impact.

Fig 6.13 (opposite) The shaft on the ground indicates ball position for the 7 Iron pitch-and-run shot.

The 7 Iron pitch-and-run — the money shot

We have practised a few specialist shots which require a high level of skill. Now we will try a very practical shot and a simple one, one that you should use as often as you possibly can — the 7 Iron pitch-and-run shot.

Think of this shot as a long putt. Aim the clubface once again at the target. Play the ball well back in the stance and just swing the club up and down the line, keeping the back of your left hand going to the target. Try this practice routine: hold the club so that the shaft is in the position shown in Fig 6.13. If you swing and flick your wrists, or turn it over, the shaft will strike off your side. To prevent this happening you must school yourself into leading with your hands. Lock the clubhead once again to the target. Play this shot as often as you can as it is a relatively safe shot. Remember, there is a 'jingle' in this shot.

▶ ESSENTIALS

1. Keep telling yourself you have a great short game — even convince your friends! Act as if you already are a great short-game player.

2. Check the position of your right-hand grip. Ensure that you are not fisting it. 'Finesse' the ball with your fingers.

3. Alignment — clubface to flag.

4. Practise, practise, practise your short game (even in your garden!).

Remember, 65 per cent of golf is your short game. If you were running your own business and one client was responsible for 65 per cent of all your custom, how well would you look after that client?

MEMBERSHIP DRIVE
Cypress Point, USA, an ultra-private club, is reported to have only 240 members. It sees almost no play. Bob Hope, a member for forty years, is reported to have said, 'One year we had a big membership drive — and drove out fifty members!'

PUTTING

A GAME WITHIN A GAME

Putting is one part of golf where the golf-ball never leaves the ground. Forty-three per cent of the shots you take during a round of golf will be on the green. The putt is the shot that demands precise accuracy. You don't need strength to strike the ball on the green, so there is no excuse for you not being a good putter. It is the one area of the game which should allow you to say to Jack Nicklaus or Nick Faldo or any of the greats: 'Let's see if I can take you on the putting green.'

Golf was not always played towards a 'hole'. Early Dutch players aimed the ball towards a stick in the ground. The stick was continually being removed by 'unseen' hands and, having eventually tired of replacing it, the players simply played the ball into the hole that remained. There are many players today who would wish the sticks used at that time had been bigger! The actual size of the golf hole is four and a half inches (11.5cms) wide. It is the same size as a cigarette packet. If someone were to ask you to strike a ball and hit a cigarette packet from a radius of two to three feet (0.5m to 1m), you would have absolutely no problem. However, when we think of it as a hole in the ground, it becomes a major problem.

The American golfer Lee Trevino once said: 'You have to feel that you are a great putter in order to be one.'

▶ A 'MUST' PUTT — HOW TO PERFORM IN COMPETITION

Have you ever had to play a very important putt? A ten-foot (3m) putt in a big match at a crucial time in the round? Does the following description bring back memories?

You are standing over the ball, you are concentrating very hard, you *must* hole it. You are somehow aware of your partner's glare, the opposition have that 'hope you lip it out far away' look on their faces. You study the line again. Your body is tight. You settle on a line — you think! You strike the putt, 'wishing' it in. You are two separate people — one hoping, the other hitting.

The ball lips out. You have missed! Suddenly your whole body deflates in disappointment. You move up towards the hole and tap the ball in. Your playing partners have already charged on to the next tee. You look at the putt again and wonder what happened. What went wrong? You think, 'If only I could hit it again!' You can't resist! You place the ball in approximately the same spot. This time you are under no pressure. It doesn't really matter. You couldn't care less, and what's more, no one else could either! You knock the putt straight into the hole. You wonder, 'now, why couldn't I have done that the first time?'

Why is it you always succeed second time around? The answer — the pressure! What do I mean by the pressure? You are 'one person' second time around. You are not 'hoping' and 'hitting' the putt. You are merely hitting it. It's just like breathing, walking, talking — you never consider how you breathe, how you talk, you just get on with it. The conscious mind is missing the second time around. You are no longer afraid, no longer pleading with yourself, 'I must hole it! I must hole it! I must hole it!'. Unknowingly, when you struck the second putt with a 'devil may care' attitude, you used only the miraculous 'subconscious' mind and body as *one*. There was no division the second time. You acted before you thought. You could see the whole picture clearly. In the 'must' putt, the essence of the person (you) was trapped, unable to express itself. Your 'head' got in the way. There is a very old saying: 'If you think for too long, you'll hit it wrong!'

THE 'POSITIVE' APPROACH

You are hoping to become a great putter one day. Here is a blueprint for a new approach to putting:

1. Write down exactly how good a putter you would like to become.

Fig 7.1 If you think positively you will be surprised at the results.

2. Then get a tape recorder and record yourself making these three points:
   'From now on my worries are over.'
   'I am a successful putter.'
   'I now control my own thoughts, and only think about the positive things I 'want' to happen.

3. Now the crucial point. Act as if you already are a great putter. Say to yourself: 'I have a beautiful putter, a lovely smooth stroke. I am a wonderful putter. The ball

123

PUTTING

The secret of success in many spheres of life is to follow instinct rather than reason. To Act before you Think. This is typical of high handicappers on the green.

A friend of mine watched this man standing over a putt for six minutes. 'What in the name of heaven is he doing?' asked his playing partner. His opponent said, 'He must be praying!' His partner replied, 'I think he finished praying a while ago, he must now be waiting for a bloody answer!'

rolls beautifully for me....' This is so important. It is based on the simple premise that believing you have it is the first stage, the natural step — the physical reality follows on from this.

4. Always keep updating your script. Make a tape of it. Play it over and over to yourself, especially just before you play a round of golf. Let it all become programmed into your subconscious mind — don't *try* to listen, just listen in a relaxed way.

5. See yourself all the time as feeding your mind with positive thoughts, weeding out the negative ones. The word 'worry' comes from an Anglo-Saxon word meaning to 'choke'. So, you must not allow negative thoughts to choke your putts. Always speak positively about your putting. Programme yourself so that you will always 'think' positively.

Switch from — to +

Avoid negative thinking, golfers who condemn themselves to bad putting. As you become more positive, the hole acts like a magnet to attract good luck — putts start to drop in from all angles. Continually feed your mind with positive thoughts. Don't allow any old thought to enter and dwell in your mind — only allow positive ones to enter. If you are able to grasp this simple

Fig 7.2 The hole should act as a magnet to the ball.

approach, you have made one of the greatest discoveries of your life — that golfers can alter their scores on the green dramatically, simply by switching their thought patterns from negative to positive. Your putting score is formed by the thoughts that habitually occupy your mind.

 A FEW SIMPLE RULES

- Do not take too long looking over your putts. If you do, you will only arouse programmed fears and anxieties, which in turn will produce rigor mortis and panic.

- Never think about *how* you are going to strike any putt.

- Give your total concentration to *where* you want the ball to go.

- Understand that improvement on the green comes about, not by making a supreme effort, but by ceasing all effort. Change from 'hitting and hoping' to merely 'hitting'. Once you do this, your awareness will increase dramatically.

- Look only once at the line to the hole. That 'picture' will stay with you.

- Now trust your instinct and strike the putt. Trust yourself to 'hole' it.

The things we do best are the things we are not aware of doing. Just 'Hole the putt! Hole the putt! Hole the putt!'.

ON THE PRACTICE GREEN

Some people call putting 'a game within a game'. As you practise and become a good technician on the green, you have to ask yourself: What is the key to it? What is it that I am looking for? In the long game you are looking for accuracy and distance. On the green, you are concerned only with accuracy. Do you need leverage? No! No wrist action, no moving parts!

You must develop a sound technique. The triangle moves together. The elbows move together. The shoulders move together. The weight is forward on the left foot and stays there for the duration of the stroke. Eyes are over the ball. Stroke is 'in to out'. Backswing should be half the distance (short) of the forward stroke. This stroke is sometimes

'WHO CARES?'
The actor Jack Lemmon, playing in the Crosby USA, slashed the ball nine times before he reached the eighteenth green at Pebble Beach. As he lined up his putt for a ten, he asked his caddie, 'Which way does it break?' 'Who cares!' replied the caddie.

referred to as the pendulum method. Pick a spot in front of the line and hit the ball.

Wait for the sound of the ball dropping into the hole. Don't look up — once you've hit the ball, it's history (let's hope it goes down in the annals as one of the great putts of our time!). Try to make a loud noise with your putter at impact. Lift the putter head up after impact, holding it over the line to the hole. I believe that the forward strike must be made with the right hand. Right hand pushes right through — a short backswing with a long, long follow-through. An upswing stroke. Get the ball rolling early. A steep and choppy swing will make the ball bounce on the green and it will always come up short.

Fig 7.3 Use the 'pendulum' method while putting.

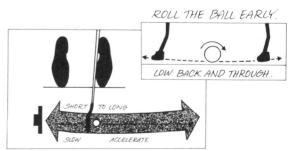

ROLL THE BALL EARLY.

LOW BACK AND THROUGH.

SHORT TO LONG

SLOW ACCELERATE

TACKLING THE COURSE

The legendary English golfer Henry Cotton once remarked: 'OK, he can strike the ball, but can he play the game?' In the final analysis, it is always the score that counts.

'I SHUDDA HAD A 63'
Two pals meet up. John has not seen Pat for a while. Pat was a keen fisherman. John enquires, 'How are you keeping and how's the fishing?' Pat replies, 'Oh, I gave up the fishing. I play the golf now and I enjoy it, like you said I would.' 'Great,' says John, 'but why did you give up the fishing?' Pat answers, 'Well, I finally realised that golf liars don't have to show anything!'

The golfer is born again every time he/she stands on the first tee. Playing a round of golf is like going on a journey. The player approaches every game with renewed optimism, in anticipation of that magic touch. Is there a secret to it all? The following will certainly help:

PREPARE WELL

Before heading off into the competition or into a game, set yourself up well. When you are having pre-game thoughts, visualise yourself playing well. Look forward to the game. Winners and losers think differently.

129

A loser sees the problem, a winner sees an opportunity. Be cautious with your club selection on the golf course. Avoid the 3 Iron, the Wood, etc, in tight lies. Once you are cautious with your selection you can afford to be optimistic about your shots.

The secret (if there is one) is to use your handicap and play within your present ability. Improve your ability only on the driving range. If you cannot pull a shot off on the practice range, don't try it on the course.

Winners and losers think differently.

It's extremely important to know when *not* to try a shot, to get into the mind of the course architect, to study the make-up of a golf course. Look at the score card — the normal card has ten par 4s, four par 3s and four par 5s. Therefore you need fourteen good tee shots, an average of fifty-six shots within a thirty yard (27m) radius of the green, and the rest long Irons and fairway Woods.

Study the indices on the score card and mark the holes where you have your shots.

If you are playing a strange course it is very important that you study the back of the card and look for local rules, like out-of-bounds areas and so forth, which may be pertinent to that particular course — the danger holes. Sometimes it is a good idea to get out and walk a few holes before the game.

Always arrive early, well before tee-off time, and hit a few shots. A friend of mine complained that he was 7 over par for the first nine holes and 1 under for the back nine. I explained to him that he had only warmed up on the back nine. If he had done his pre-game warm-up routine he would have played well throughout. The early swings in a round of golf need a lot of oil to make the swing fluid. You must think of this — your muscles will be cold and tight unless you do a warm-up.

It is also important to dress well — this will help you to feel better and, consequently, you will play better golf.

On the practice area, start with your Wedge to give your muscles a chance to warm up. Always finish with a few wooden shots because the first shot you will play will be a tee shot and a few good tee shots will set up good round.

Avoid the pitfalls on the course. Remember that each shot is the only shot you have, so you must make the right decision.

I firmly believe you have a 'deadly' short game.

► REMEMBER THE FOLLOWING POINTS:

Take advantage of the tee

When we stand on a tee we are being given an advantage — we are allowed to tee the ball up. My advice is: tee the ball up, well up in the air. When I see a player tee really low, I know instantly that he has problems. He is afraid of the high tee because his swing is too steep. If you are given an advantage in life you should always take it. Tee the ball up really high, learn to widen your swing and sweep the ball away — take it clean. Leave the tee in the ground and keep practising this. A narrow, steep swing will be quickly shown up.

Maintain a 'soft' grip on the club

When we stand on the tee, we are inclined to focus on the flag on the green. We are hypnotised by it. It seems a long distance away so we gather ourselves for a mighty effort to drive the ball an enormous distance. Force becomes an instant issue. This leads to a tighter grip and muscle tension in the body. The secret here is not to squeeze the blood out of your hands by holding too tightly. Someone once asked Arnold Palmer: 'What is inside a golf ball?' He replied: 'The centre is wrapped in rubber that is almost as tense as most golfers who try to hit it!' Muscles need blood. Bloodless hands are lifeless hands. Softly, softly with the hands, is the secret of the masters. As they say: 'Don't force the feel — feel the force.' To soften the hands, to rid them of tension, try banging them together hard, five

or six times, then go back to the club. You
will notice your hands are relaxed again. To
develop a smooth, even tempo, you need a
'soft' grip.

Favour the loft over distance

When you knock down your tee shot you
feel embarrassed and annoyed. You
instinctively feel that a superhuman effort is
required in order to amend the wrong, to
try to save the day, and so the power
syndrome takes over. My advice in this
instance is: react in the opposite way to how
you instinctively feel, and if there is a
conflict between loft and distance, always
favour loft. Under pressure, in any situation,
when things are not going the way they
should be — the machine is not working
correctly — we try to slow it down and see
what the problem is. It is the very same in
golf. If you knock down a tee shot into
semi-rough, you should probably take out a
7 or 8 Iron and play the ball down the
fairway. A keen golfer friend of mine
revealed the secret behind his Captain's Prize
win by telling me that he never played for
the green. If he missed the small green the
hazards were very severe. So he played his
second shot up in front of the green and
his left him with a very straightforward
third shot. He out-foxed the golf course.
Golf is a thinking person's game. As the
saying goes: 'The six inches between the ears
are the most important.'

'Sweep' the wood away

The wooden shot is your first shot. The
wood is a flat-faced club. You have got to
avoid a 'V' type swing (see chapter 1). A lot

of the great players adopt a slightly closed stance on the drive. (See Fig 8.1.) This means that their right foot is back and the left foot is forward. They are thinking about

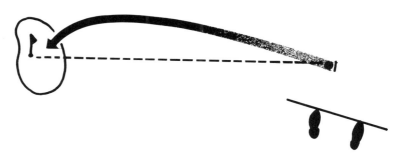

a 'wide' type of swing, looking at the back of the ball and creating width, and holding it. In other words, sweeping the ball clean and leaving the tee in the ground. You must learn to strike the wood on your upswing.

Fig 8.2 Hit the ball with the Driver on the upswing for maximum distance.

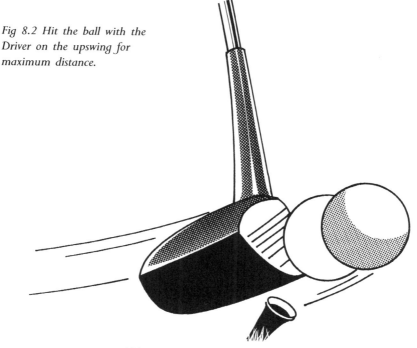

'Delicate' power gives results

Your tempo is very, very important in golf. If you are driving a nail into wood, an accurate strike with the hammer is much more effective than a massive stroke. (See Fig 2.10.) So it is with golf. A good, even tempo, working the machine and hitting the ball accurately, will drive the ball enormous distances.

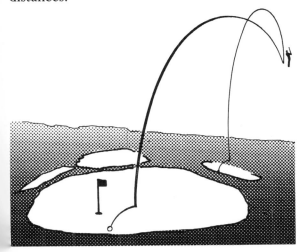

Fig 8.3 A lot of golfers think they are stronger than they actually are! They are disappointed when the ball lands short in the bunker. If this happens to you, try using one extra club, for example, an 8 rather than a 9 Iron.

Know your clubs

This is also very important. For example, avoid playing a 3 Iron off a tight lie. A 5 Wood or a 7 Wood is much easier. As a general rule you should put your pride in your pocket if you want to win. Play with the club you are happiest with, and play the shot you feel will lead you closer to the pin – whatever that may be. A 130-yard (119m) shot could be a punch with a 6 Iron — it doesn't always have to be a full 9 Iron.

Avoid the 'common' errors

In their approach shots to the green, golfers make two fundamental errors:

Fig 8.4 Do not become hypnotised by the flag. Play for the centre of the green and you will have better results.

1. They are hypnotised by the flag and tend to go directly for it instead of looking on the green as a whole, complete unit. You should play for the centre of the green most of the time. (See Fig 8.4.)

2. The second common fault is under-clubbing — coming up short. Always play an attacking shot past the pin. Another fault allied to this is over-swinging and a tendency to 'fluff' the ball. I always tell golfers: you will never get a medal for striking a 9 Iron 150 yards (137m) but you might get a prize if you can land the ball on the centre of the green near the flag. There are no medals for distance in golf!

GOLF IS A THREE MINUTE GAME!

A lot of golfers put themselves under undue pressure, especially beginners. They try to concentrate all the time during the round — they tend to mix up concentration with tension. You may spend four hours playing a round of golf and at least another hour talking about it in the bar, but it takes only two seconds to play each stroke. So you are playing golf for approximately three minutes! It is during these three minutes that you should focus on the round of golf.

Fig 8.5 Try not to think of what might go wrong with your shot. Instead, use 'narrow vision' and focus on the middle of the green.

Concentration is seeing the shot and playing it without interference from the conscious mind, like breathing, talking, etc. Act before you think!

You only need to concentrate as you are playing the shot — in between times you should relax. I call this 'narrow vision' and 'wide vision'. As you walk down the fairway

Fig 8.6 To get correct alignment, you must aim the clubhead directly at the target and align your body parallel to the left of the target.

you should have wide vision, take it all in. You might check out parallel holes, smell the flowers. As the charismatic American golfer Walter Hagen once said on the way round: 'As you arrive at your ball, change to narrow vision, go behind the ball, see the shot.'

Know your distance — you should know to within a few feet exactly how far you should strike each shot with each club. Develop a personal Distance Chart. There is only the ball and the green. You aim the scoring part of the club, the clubhead, at the target and you sweep the ball to it. See the tunnel. Once you have played the shot, relax again and revert back to wide vision.

ACT AS IF YOU ALREADY ARE A GOOD GOLFER!

To really enjoy golf, you must have inner confidence. Quietly remind yourself that you are a good player, that you enjoy the game, that you like practising, that you have a great short game. Always wish the very best to your opponents. Be big. Play the course rather than your opponent. Encourage your playing partner and wish him/her well. Compliment them on a good shot. If you are a beginner you should study etiquette. A lot of it is common sense — respect for your golfing friends and for the golf course. Become a brisk player. Don't be too hard on yourself! — as a beginner, when you are not playing in competitions, tee the ball up if you are out on the fairway.

► DEVELOP A ROUTINE

One cannot stress enough the importance of developing a routine on the golf course, and you can do this by practising setting up to the ball in exactly the same way every time. Try to repeat everything you do, even the way you walk. Take your time, walk slowly and do exactly the same in each golf game — get into a routine. Your swing will become routine and your play will become more consistent.

► HOW TO SCORE WELL IN WINDY CONDITIONS

You can judge the wind in several ways: observe the trees, flag or pin, or toss a pinch of grass into the air. Alternatively, learn from other players' shots.

Into the wind: Take a less lofted club than usual. Aim the clubhead at the target and into the wind. Always position your body ahead of the ball — opposite your right foot.

Fig 8.7 a) When playing against the wind use a less lofted club and play the ball back in your stance; b) When playing with the wind use a more lofted club and position the ball forward in your stance.

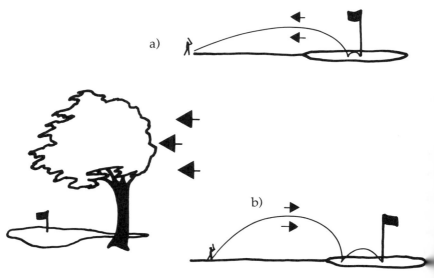

Move the weight onto your left foot and play the shot by swinging the hook of your left hand to the target. Play past the pin.

With the wind: Use a more lofted club than normal. Tee the ball higher. If driving, you could use a 3 Wood to get the ball airborne. It will go just as far as the Driver. Aim the clubhead at your target, play the ball forward in your stance, keep the weight back on your right foot, hit the ball 'up to heaven', and hit the ball with the clubhead on the upswing.

In a crosswind: Take a less lofted club than usual. Allow for the wind to affect the ball's flight and aim the clubhead at the intended target. If the wind is against you, try to keep the ball down. If the wind is helping you, try to get the ball up into the wind and use it to your advantage.

In windy conditions you should generally use your hands more, go for a 'wristier' swing, and if there are gale force winds on the green you must tap the putt using a stroke. Adopt the Byron Nelson motto: *'Make the wind your friend.'* Generally adopt a wider than normal stance in order to anchor yourself. Try to swing less and hit more.

HOW TO PLAY FROM UNEVEN LIES

You will come up against uneven lies on the golf course. Generally speaking, if the hill is going away from you and you are standing above the ball, the flight will also go away from you — the ball will go left to right. (See Fig 8.8(a).) If the hill is coming back towards you, the ball will tend to go right to left. (See Fig 8.8(b).) In these instances you must make sure you take plenty of loft in the club and make allowances. If the ball is

a)

b)

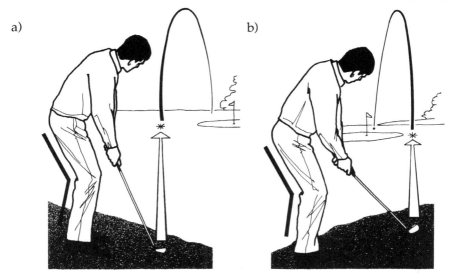

Fig 8.8
a) Side-hill lie
When you play from the side of a hill and the ball is below your feet, make sure you aim to the left of the target, as the ball will travel from left to right.

b) *When the ball is above your feet aim to the right of the target, as the ball will travel from right to left.*

below your feet you have to aim left; if the ball is above your feet, aim right. When confronted with a shot from an uneven lie, avoid a full swing, that is, a driving range one. Waggle the clubhead, allow for the slope and flick the ball away. Play a 'hands only' shot.

Above all, approach your golf with the correct mentality. I will leave you with a number of what I consider to be key points in this regard:

1. You must have a repetitive thought pattern. In other words, you can't be in a dither going out to play golf — forget it.

2. Picture the shot mentally before swinging a club. The better the picture of the shot in the mind, the greater the chance of

accomplishing it. Your attitude must be one of expectation, not of doubt. When putting, for example, picture yourself actually picking the ball out of the hole.

3. Make a list of a few key swing thoughts. Choose one key thought each day and concentrate positively on it. It is impossible to contend with more than one key idea at any one time.

4. Watch your alignment (see Fig 8.6.) It is just as important to think about tactics as about swing. How often have you seen a golfer making a perfect swing but never taking account of the alignment? He aims in the wrong direction or takes the wrong club. He hits a great shot but ends up either thirty yards (27m) short of or forty yards (36m) past the green.

5. In developing your own particular style, try to model yourself on some player who has the same stature as yourself.

6. Always relax between each shot. It can help to ameliorate or alter particular problems which arise between shots. It is to your advantage if you can direct your mind away from the pressure of the moment. Tension can pose difficulties for the golfer. I'd like to share with you a little ploy which you may find helpful. Before you strike the ball, tighten every muscle as hard as you can, gripping the club with all your might. Then relax. If you use this formula it will help dispel pent-up tension in the system. You will then be 'ready to play'.

143

'WHAT DOG?'
This story exemplifies the terror that consumes most amateurs when playing tournament golf.

The actor Jack Lemmon was about to drive when out of the gallery tore a big scruffy dog. It ran straight through Lemmon's legs and disappeared into the crowd on the other side of the tee. Without batting an eye, Lemmon played a fine tee shot.

Jim Demaret, doing commentary after the round, went up to Jack and said, 'Jack, that was really remarkable composure you displayed back there on the fifteenth tee. That dog ran right between your legs and you didn't let it disturb you at all!'

Lemmon looked at Demaret in complete surprise, and said, 'You mean that was a real dog?'

7. Will power and determination are fundamental ingredients in effecting positive progress in your performance. Perhaps it is this quality of will power which marks the demarcation line between the great and the ordinary. As the American psychologist Emerson once said: *'They conquer who believe they can.'*

TWO TYPICAL GOLF LESSONS

Lesson 1

PROBLEM

The slice

ADVICE

Correct the slice by changing the set-up, not the swing

APPENDIX

When a golfer comes to me with a major swing problem, I do not try to change his or her swing. Rather, I change the set-up, as a result of which the player will make (or be forced to make) a completely different swing.

It's as simple as this. A player tells me, 'My problem is that all my shots are high and right, I have a terrible slice.' I know that his swing-plane is much too steep, his angle of attack on the ball is from the outside down, and the actual clubface is 'open' to the swing-line at impact. I explain the need to **change the angle of attack** from 'above' to 'behind', the need for a **more inside, wider backswing,** avoiding the quick left. His tension grip is ruining any chance of a smooth swing. I tell him: 'Do you know that you are gripping so hard, you are squeezing the blood out of your hands and the life out of your game.' If he wants a tidy game he must have a **light grip.** Above all he must **'knuckle down',** that is, show more knuckles on his left hand. This grip change will alter the clubface angle automatically. I insist that he set his left side much higher than his right side — drop his right shoulder down and tuck in his right elbow. Finally, I change his stance from an open to a closed one.

Every angle has altered. All roads lead one way. I have trapped his body into a position whereby the only escape route is from the inside out. His new (awkward) body position will block any attempt at the outside-in route. The grip change will close the clubface at impact.

I insist that he uses a no. 7 iron and 'tees' the ball up.

Here is the sequence:
- GRIP: change left-hand grip to show more knuckles
- FOCUS on back rather than top of ball (more inside)
- STANCE: closed (again more inside)

Swing/backswing
- Turn more inside
- 'Hood' the clubface on the way back and extend triangle.

Forward swing
- Clear the left side
- Close the door; rotate right hand over impact.
- Do not hit the ball any more, instead learn to 'hook' it down the fairway.

Lesson 2

PROBLEM   **ADVICE**
Lack of distance Increase the distance by
adding 'leverage' to the
swing.

A golfer comes to me for a lesson. She is
unhappy with her game. She is elderly and
associates the 'ageing' process with her loss
of distance. I know instantly that her swing
lacks 'leverage'. The problem is compounded
by the fact that the more distance she
loses, the more she feels she must force the
shot. Hence she makes a violent attack on
the ball. The swing is very short, hurried,
steep, and a frustrating one with little return
for the 'effort' involved.

I always start the lesson by asking 'Do you
know you have a clubhead?', and to drive
the point home I say, 'You know it's not an
ornament you have at the end of the stick.' I
stress the need to **regard the club as a
machine.** The grip end is only the 'holding
end', the clubhead end is the 'working end'.
I tell her she must **'work the stick'** a lot
more, to manipulate, to activate the
clubhead end. If you consider your hands for
a moment, it is very obvious that the fingers
have far more manipulative powers than the
palms. I insist on her achieving **much more
'finger grip',** to knuckle down — a lighter,
lower finger grip. I demonstrate the 'bending
the shaft' on the ball by strong
'waggling' of the clubhead — bending the
lower end of the shaft.

I encourage her to **swing more,** to increase the length of her backswing by excessive wrist-work, to 'overswing'. I show her how the swing is 'pumped' — how power is pumped into the swing. I egg her along with phrases like 'Your old swing made you look as if you were in a phone box!', 'You are in such a hurry to swipe the ball...you must be double parked outside the range!' and 'If you are going to miss it...you might as well miss it with a good swing!' All the time I am endeavouring to unlock her swing, to unlock the power so that it can be released on the forward swing.

On the forward swing, above all I encourage her to really let that clubhead go at the ball through impact, to feel the clubhead win the race to the ball. I show her the **ideal impact position** — the clubhead is way ahead of the hands at impact. It is as if somebody has hooked her hands back at impact, pulled the handle back and allowed the head fly through. You only need power *once* in the golf swing — at impact. The strong right hand can be a killer in the backswing, but **strength is a tremendous asset if you use it at the right time.** I demonstrate the right forearm 'power kick' at impact.

A longer, slower, freer swing will become self-generating and powerful. Sam Snead once remarked that to play your best golf 'you must feel that your wrists are oily'.

'QUIT WHILE YOU'RE AHEAD'

Pine Valley is probably the toughest golf course in the world. It is often referred to as a 184-acre bunker. It terrifies golfers.

Woody Platt, a gifted local amateur, started on the toughest course, a par 4, 427 yards (390.5m), and managed a birdie 3. This was no easy task as the hole bends sharply to the right after the tee shot to a green that drops steeply into trouble on both sides and to the rear. He played a 4 Iron second shot.

Hole two, 367 yards (335.5m). The tee shot must carry 180 yards of sand peppered with flash-traps along its right side. The green of course is elevated and completely surrounded by sandy wasteland. Woody hit a 7 Iron second shot directly onto the hole for an eagle 2. (Three under after two holes.)

Par 3, 185 yards (169m). Strictly a one-shotter as there is nothing between the tee and the green but sand, sand, sand. The green tilts sharply from right to left downhill. If the player misses this green, a 6 or 7 is possible. Woody solved the problem by the single expedient of a hole-in-one. (Five under the card.)

Hole four is a very long par 4, 461 yards (421.5m). A blind tee shot with the hole swerving very sharply to the right. There is sand everywhere. Woody Platt struck a Driver and 4 Iron and then holed a thirty-footer for a birdie. (Six under the card on one of the toughest golf courses in the world.)

The first four holes make a full circle back to the clubhouse. Woody now faced the prospect of playing the fifth, one of the toughest par 3 courses in the world. A huge bunker lies in front of the green, falling steeply to the right onto saplings and undergrowth. As the hole is 226 yards (206.5m) long, he would have to play a Driver. Before proceeding, he decided he needed to bolster his spirits with a drink in the clubhouse while he contemplated the task ahead.

He never came out of the clubhouse! This is a true story.

GLOSSARY OF GOLFING TERMS

Ace
The ultimate stroke in golf, a hole in one.

Albatross
A hole completed in three strokes under par.

Arc
The path which the club takes through the swing.

Better-ball
A game in which two partners play as a team and the best score is counted. Also called *four-ball*.

Birdie
A hole completed in one stroke under par.

Blind (hole or shot)
A blind hole is one where the green cannot be seen from the tee. A blind shot is made when a high object prevents the player from seeing where he/she intends to hit the ball.

Bogey
A hole completed in one stroke over par. A double-bogey is a hole completed in two strokes over par, and so on.

Bunker
A hazard filled with sand.

Bye
The number of holes left to be played when a match is finished.

Caddie
A person who carries the player's clubs.

Casual water
A temporary pool of water on the golf course. When the course is waterlogged after heavy rain, the player is permitted to lift and drop the ball clear without penalty if is lying in casual water.

Chip
short shot to the green.

Concede
hole is conceded when one player has played so many ots that it is impossible for him/her to win or halve it th the opponent. A player may also concede the ponent's putt if he/she feels that the opponent is certain t to miss. Concessions take place only in match-play.

Dead
Used to describe the situation when the ball lands so near the hole that it is all but impossible for the player to miss the putt.

Divot
The piece of turf that is sometimes removed when the ball is struck. All divots should be replaced to avoid damage to the course.

Dormie
In match-play, a player is dormie if he/she is as many holes ahead as there are holes left to play, for example, if a player were three holes ahead with three to play, then this player would be dormie three.

Draw
The spin imparted to the ball so that it moves gradually from right to left.

Eagle
A hole completed in two strokes under par.

Fade
The spin imparted to the ball so that it moves gradually from left to right.

Fairway
The cut portion of the course between the teeing ground and the green.

Flagstick
The pole, usually with a small flag attached, that is placed in the hole to provide the player with a target. Also called the *pin*.

Fluffed shot
When the player strikes too much ground.

Fore
A shout of warning to anyone on the golf course indicating that the ball is travelling in their direction.

Four-ball
See BETTER-BALL.

Foursome
A form of golf with two partners per team, but instead of playing their own ball as in better-ball, the partners play alternate shots with the same ball and drive at alternate holes.

Free drop
Under certain conditions a player is allowed to drop the ball away without penalty. Check the rules of golf if in doubt.

Green
Each putting surface on the course.

Greensome
A form of foursome in which two players play as a team but each player drives and then the team decides which ball to play in alternate strokes for the remainder of the hole.

Grip
The position of the hands on the club and also the top part of the club where the hands are placed, which is usually covered in rubber or leather.

Ground under repair
Ground which has been repaired by the green-keeper. The area is usually marked by a small notice.

Halved
A hole is halved, or a match is halved, when the opponents are level, either in relation to strokes taken at each hole or at the end of a round.

Handicap
The figure allotted to every player, denoting the average difference between his/her score and the par of the course.

Hanging lie
A downhill lie.

Hazard
A bunker, ditch, stream or pond.

Hole
The target on the green into which the ball must ultimately fall. The hole is 4½ inches (11.43cm) in diameter. Also refers to the full distance between tee and green.

Holing-out
Striking the ball into the hole.

Honour
The preference given to the player whose turn it is to drive first. The honour on the first tee can be agreed, but thereafter it goes to the player who had the lowest score at the previous hole. If a hole is halved, the player with the honour retains it.

Hook
A shot which moves sharply in flight from right to left.

Hosel
The point at which the shaft of the club enters the clubhead.

Knuckle down
Term used to describe the four-knuckle grip.

Ladies' tee
The teeing ground used by women golfers, usually placed some distance ahead of the men's tee.

Lateral water hazard
A ditch or stream which, when viewed from the fairway, runs parallel to a hole instead of across it.

Lift and drop under penalty
If a ball has to be lifted because it is impossible to play it from where it lies, the player is permitted to lift and drop under the penalty laid down by the rules.

Local rules
The rules of golf apply everywhere the game is played, but all clubs have additional rules on certain points pertaining to the layout of the course.

Loft
The angle at which the clubhead lies in relation to the shaft.

Lost ball
Players are allowed five minutes to look for a lost ball, after which time they have to deem the ball lost and play another.

Match-play
When players play against each other individually or as a team.

Medal-play
When the player counts the number of strokes taken during the round. Also called *stroke-play*.

Niblick
A golf-club with a heavy head and wide face, used for lofting.

Obstructions
Objects, either movable or immovable, which prevent the playing of a shot.

Out of bounds
When the ball is hit over the boundaries of the course or hole, thus incurring a penalty.

Outside agency
Any person or animal not involved in the game who obstructs or moves the ball.

Par
The rating allocated to a hole or to a course, based on the terrain, the length of the hole and the level of difficulty.

Partner
The person with whom one plays.

Penalty
When a shot finishes in a lie from which the ball is unplayable, out of bounds or lost, then a penalty is incurred according to the rules. Penalties can also be incurred for infringement of the rules.

Pitch
A high, lofted shot played from near the green.

Playing out of turn
In match-play, if a golfer plays out of turn either from the tee or fairway, then the opponent may request that the ball be called back and the shot played again.

Playing preferred lies
See WINTER RULES

Power fade
Long shot which flies slightly to the right at the end.

Pull
A shot that flies directly to the left with no slice-spin; to hit a shot directly to the left with no hook-spin.

Push
A shot that flies directly to the right with no slice-spin; to hit a shot directly to the right with no hook-spin.

Putt
The stroke used on the greens and played with a putter.

Round
To play a round is to complete all the holes on the course, usually eighteen.

Rub of the green
Interference with the ball that is attributed to fate.

Score-card
The card that is filled in by golfers in stroke-play. It has to be filled in by the player's partner, and checked and signed by both players.

Set-up
The player's position at address.

Shank shot
Ball struck with the shank of the club.

Short game
The term used to describe shots played in the vicinity of the green.

Sky shot
Very high shot.

Slice
A shot which moves sharply in flight from left to right.

Stroke
The striking of the ball.

Stroke-play
See MEDAL-PLAY.

Swing-line
The direction of the swing.

Swing-plane
Angle of swing in relation to the ground.

Take-away
Backswing.

Tee
The wooden or plastic peg on which the ball is placed prior to driving off. Also the teeing ground.

Tee-markers
Metal or plastic objects used to mark the forward limits of the teeing ground.

Tempo
Speed of swing.

Through the green
The term used in referring to the whole area of the course *except* the teeing ground, the putting green and all hazards on the course. The term is also used when a player hits a shot too boldly so that it runs over the back of the green.

Top
Ball runs along ground.

Trap
Also called a bunker.

Winter rules
Special rules for play during the months when the course is wet or frost-bound. Winter rules allow for the ball to be lifted and cleaned and then replaced adjacent to its original position but not nearer to the hole, without penalty — thereby lessening the damage to the course. Also referred to as 'playing preferred lies'.